Ecological Metabolism:
In Pursuit of Landscape's
Equality in the Urban Realm

Carla Novak

I0502732

Ecological Metabolising / Novak, Carla
ISBN Number: 978-1-291-04607-6

© Carla Novak

All attempts have been made to identify owners of copyright.

January 2011

The town planners and
gardeners are continuously
keeping ecology from
flourishing by placing
boundaries and pruning

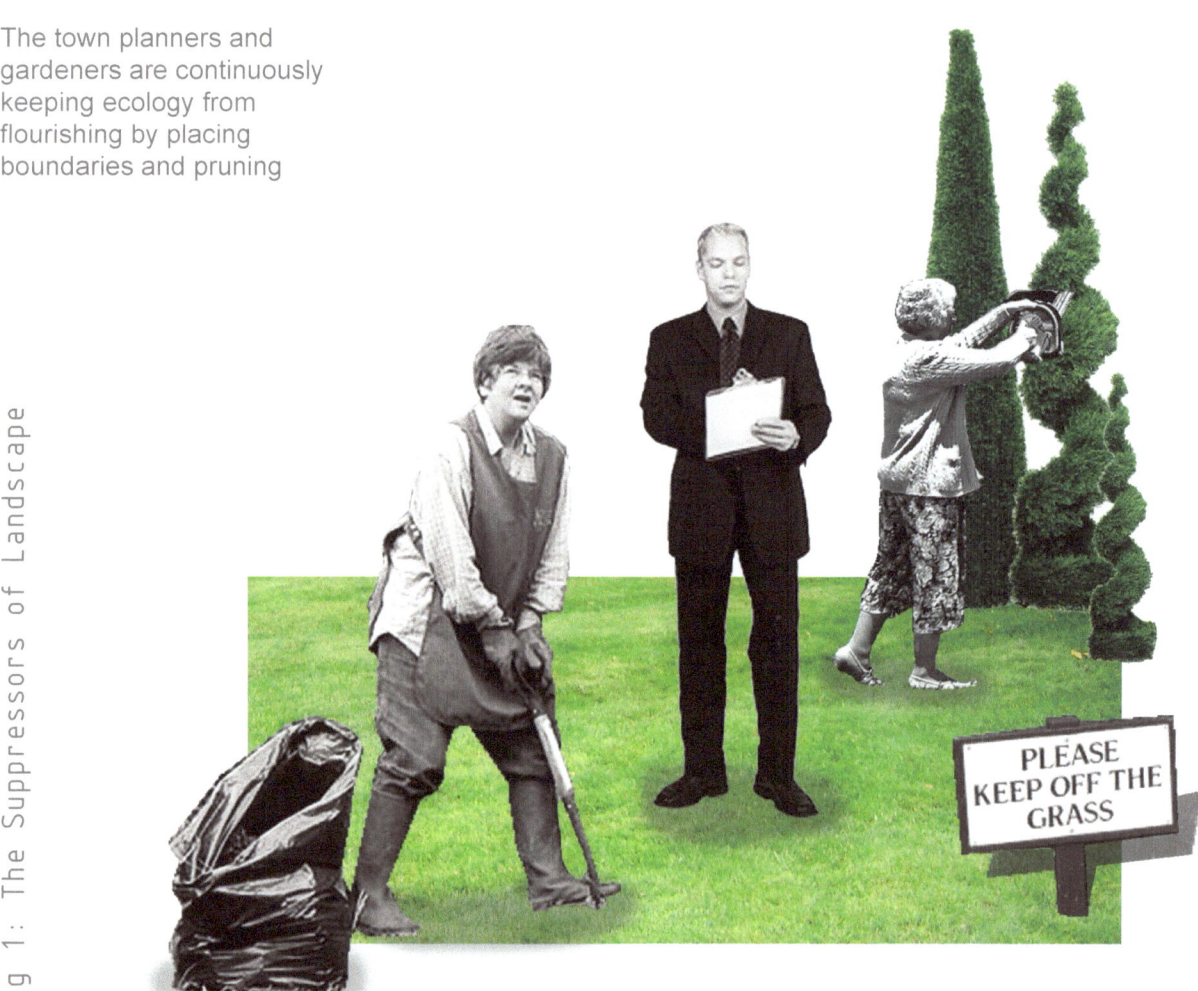

Fig 1: The Suppressors of Landscape

PLEASE
KEEP OFF THE
GRASS

Gardeners are the suppressors of Landscape in the urban realm: their continuous de-heading and pruning confines landscape to the idealistic regimentation of planning authorities and residential gardening committees. The stifling of the latent potential of Landscape's ecological thickness (Allen 2002) by the overzealous human control of self-generating landscape urbanism, and its banishment to the familiarity of such urbanistic typologies as the 'park' and 'public square', restricts landscape's occupation of anything other than the ground plane (beyond merely gestural green roofs and walls etc) in strictly maintained areas, limiting Landscape's potentially important role within the city. With much of Landscape in the city reduced to over-defined public space controlled by borders of paths, iron railings and planters, or through symbolic gestures (rather than active catalysts) of sustainability, Landscape needs to break free from its restraints and be allowed to interact with the urban fabric.

There is a predisposition toward landscape as inherently positive and urbanism as negative, identifiable perhaps as *'symbolic rurality'* (Howard 2007), whereby *'more than half of us feel the need to be closer to the country and rural life, and nine out of ten people want to be close to nature'* (ibid). However, James Corner considers an integration of the two, stating that *'the union of landscape with urbanism promises new relational and systemic workings across territories of vast scale and scope'* (2006:33), and that both might learn and take on attributes of each other in driving the future of urbanism forward. With rising populations in cities set to continue, maintaining the traditional notion of landscape as something competing with rather than working in conjunction with urbanism will lead to a failure of architects and urban planners to make any *'significant contributions to future urban formations'* (2006:30).

The prevention of this merging process is rigidly enforced by the notion within the city of 'landscape' as a foreign body of which we should be wary; any concept of not maintaining the greenery present in our cities is seen as morally and civically reckless. Presently, Landscape and the city are viewed as separate entities, and the urbanist maintains endless control within the city.

However, there are surfaces and territories in the city that could be used as potential sites for landscape to break free of its confinement to controlled enclaves across the ground-plane; Landscape could reach its potential to define new types of space and change the way we view and use the city.

London is a great model of Landscape's restrictions - the green space is bound by rules of the Georgian-era residential squares and council restrictions. London needs a regenerative model to follow, encouraging the exploration of the diversity and integration that landscape could introduce to the city. It is possible that by considering the scale of these tactics, looking at the smaller territories of London's urban voids, we might investigate the physical and political restrictions we put up to control the blurring of these two layers and, in this way, *'expand notions, deny boundaries [and] discover unnamable hybrids'* (Koolhaas:1994:970). Also noteworthy is the ecological potential for different organisms to share the green spaces of the city.

Allowing the landscape to manipulate the network of buildings will create public areas and points of interaction as important in-between space. The traditional role of pastoral green space in urban environments is to convey a feeling of fresh air and a healthy atmosphere in the congestion of the urban realm; *'Cities are seen to be busy with the technology of high density building, transportation infrastructures, [...] and various forms of social stress; whereas landscape, in the form of parks,[...] and gardens, is generally seen to provide both salve and respite from the deleterious effects of urbanism'* (Corner 2006:22). However, Corner proposes that there should be an overlap of the two; that urban spaces can become entwined with landscape and concomitantly effect and mediate the city.

The notion that landscape can work in balance with the urban environment might create interconnected spaces that *'contribute to the overall health and well-being of the urban population.'* (Allen 2006:22). As Stan Allen and Corner believe, a union of landscape and urbanism can create *'new relational and systemic workings across territories of vast scale and scope'* (Allen 2006:33). Thus, green-space and its inherent ecology is not just 'placed' into the urban realm as gestural pseudo-rurality, (for example in London's Royal Parks), but woven into the infrastructure of the city, blurring the edges of landscape and urbanism.

Many architects and planning authorities have utilised Landscape as a tool for instigating 'sustainability', and for demarcating public spaces and façade decoration, using *'Biodiversity'* (Bishop 2007:25) as a function of appearing to create a sustainable city. CJ Lim's *Smartcities* considers the sustainable aspect of nature by introducing ecology into the city as a working tool for growing and harvesting food for the public, thus increasing sustainability and improving urbanism for future generations *'Smartcity is a vision of how the city of the 21st Century*

CJ Lim's Smartcities utilised ecology as a
mode of sustainability

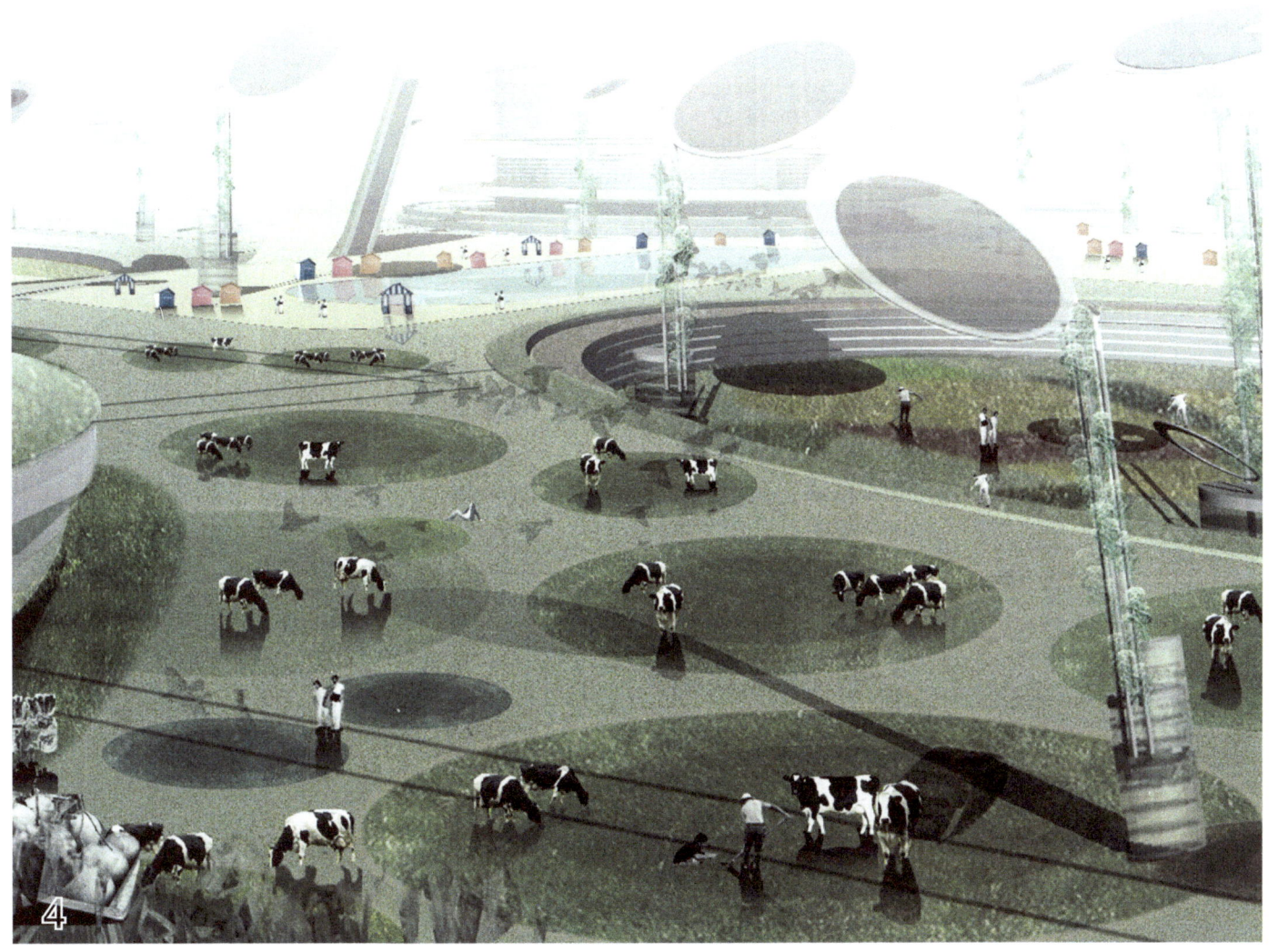

might appear of we are serious about living sustainably and wish to leave any form of legacy to our descendants.' (Lim 2010:7) Although this approach suggests themes of Landscape Urbanism, the landscape still exists only in containments. Landscape Urbanism could indeed be used for growing food, but to limit landscape as a resource, instead of leaving it to the freedom of interpretation, creates boundaries of what one can and can't do upon the Landscape surface.

Corner proposed projects like the New York High Line as an example of Landscape Urbanism, combining the two into a public space with interventions of architecture nestled into landscape. However, I feel the potential of the site was missed by Field Operations, as the intriguing occurrence of natural life that inspired the project in the first place, was destroyed during construction of the park. Whilst appearing as 'light intervention' upon completion, Field operations physical tactics were actually quite heavy- handed. The existing naturally-developed ecology was replaced with an artificial landscape that mimicked the original in many ways, but was to every extent a replacement. The plants and bushes that had naturally appeared between the rails were replaced with new ones, contained within hard surfaces and man-made textures.

In turning this self-seeded green space into a 'public park', and by destroying the ecology that had begun to transform an abandoned infrastructural surface, Corner contradicts the motions set out in *Terra Fluxus* and falls into the trap of containing Landscape within the safe and familiar urban typology of the 'park' (Corner 2006:32). If instead of replacing the existing plantation with new socially acceptable plants, they had 'embraced the weed' and allowed it to flourish into an adaptive strip of pasture that weaved through the city, the project would have been more successful in showing the potential of allowing ecology to activate spaces and surfaces.

If we adjusted our judgment of weeds and climbers (which, when left to grow, flourish into impressive meadows) and the oppression of ecology with over-active pruning and weed spraying, we could then let Landscape define its own role within the urban realm. Taking Landscape beyond gestural sustainability and breaking out of the public space, it can flourish out of its boundaries. This can create a networked urbanism, were Landscape and Urbanism blend into one another and boundaries between them become diminished. This process could give rise to new programmes in the city, or to the reactivation of existing areas.

5

There are many boundaries that we are encased in everyday: skin, clothes, rooms, doors, buildings etc. These boundaries, in an urban context, turn into networks in and around the city, 'Boundaries define

The High Line before any construction took place, the planting that inspired the project still in place

Construction underway, diggers rip out existing ecology and tracks

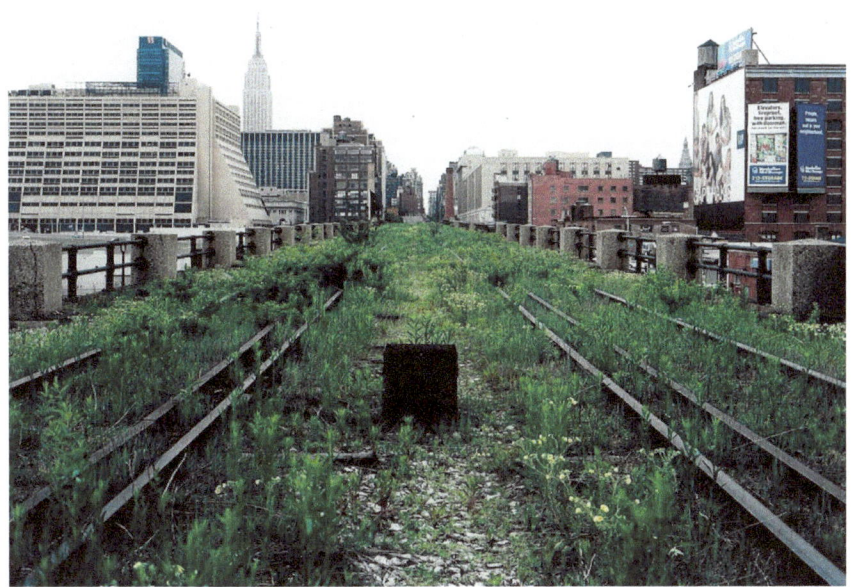

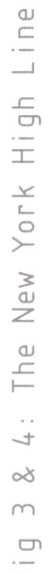

Fig 3 & 4: The New York High Line

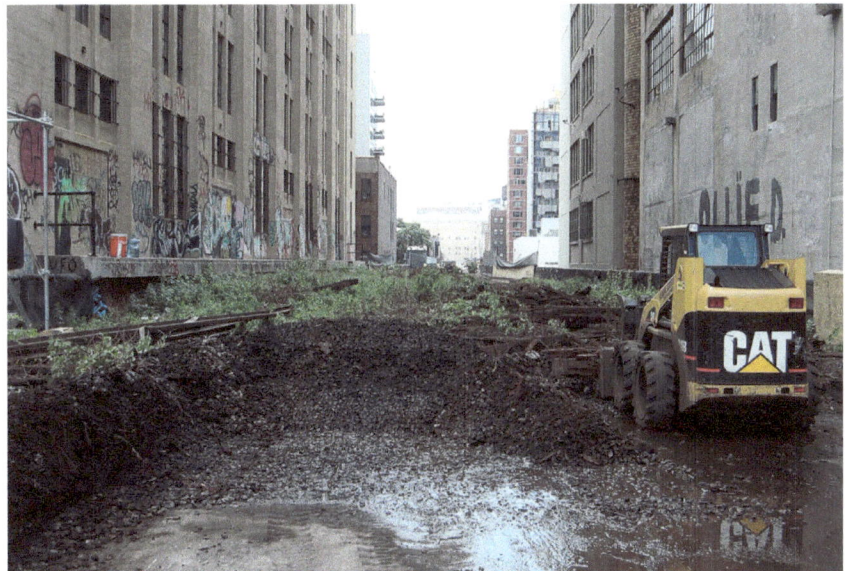

6

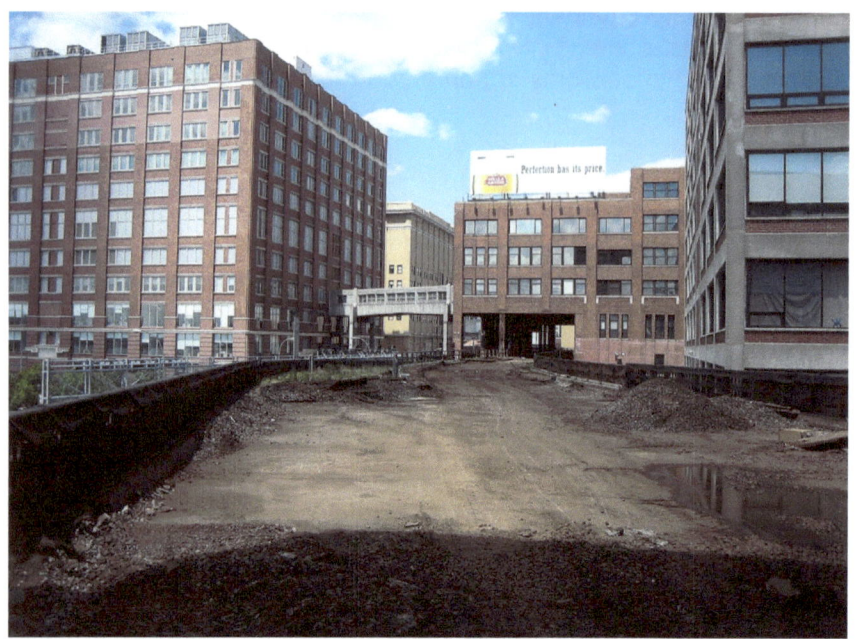

The High Line once it has been cleared of all ecology

The High Line as it stand now. An artificial surface has been placed and foliage place to appear as a natural occurrence

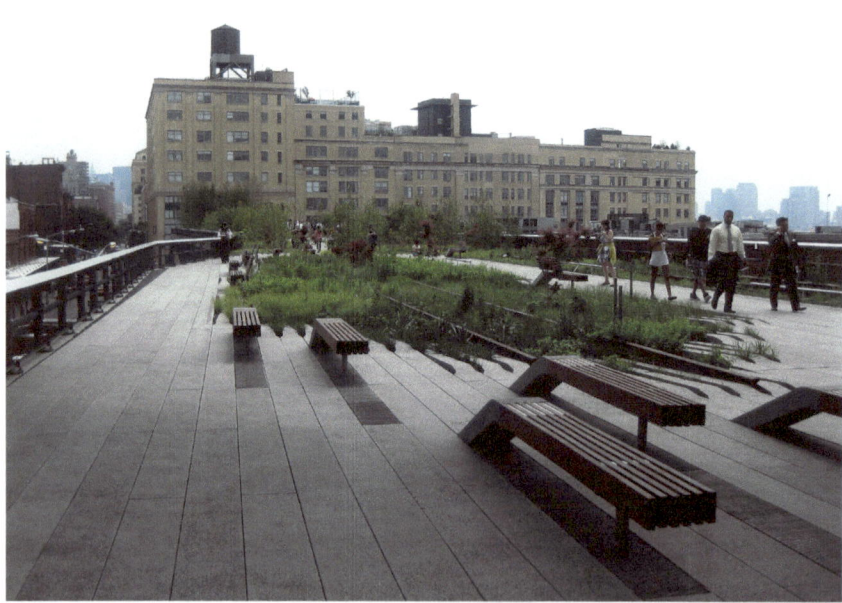

Fig 5 & 6: The New York High Line

There are many boundaries that we are encased in everyday: skin, clothes, rooms, doors, buildings etc. These boundaries, in an urban context, turn into networks in and around the city, *'boundaries define a space of container and places, while networks establish a space of links and flows. Walls, fences and skin divides, while paths, pipes and wires connect.'* (Mitchell 2003:7) This allows us to observe the city as a grid, observing the networks of spaces between its modular components. London has strict boundaries of town planning with controlled borders defining public spaces, green space and parks, creating a network of town house terraces around semi-public 'squares' that spread across much of the capital during it's 18th-19th Century expansion, resulting in *'multiple public spaces embedded in networks or streets and avenues.'* (Mitchell 2003:154) From above, the city's main focus is the territories of landscaped gardens and architecture. However, the level of control seems to over-shadow and restrict the occupation of these public spaces and the landscapes contained within them, projecting the impression that, in this instance, *'Urban public spaces are authoritarian for suppressing people'* (Nishizawa 2010:144). In an attempt to keep out 'undesirables' and recreate areas of pastoral countryside where one might 'escape' the city, these spaces become separated from the urban realm they are supposed to benefit, and from the people that might activate them. Times have changed since this particular era of urban development; *'our habitats no longer consist of single or contiguous enclosures, but have become increasingly fragmented and dispersed'* (Mitchell 2003:16). Therefore the model of the enclosed Georgian square needs re-opening to the city within which its form is so prevalent. We should learn to embrace our new sociological dynamics as *'life cannot be contained within a single lot. People's sense of living expands beyond it, effectively erasing all borders'* (Nishizawa 2010:98).

London needs to metabolise beyond the *'urban grain'* (Sudjic 2007:266) that it has grown accustomed to. If we consider the theories of metabolism initiated by Kisho Kurokawa in the 1960s and subsequently augmented by Koh Kitayama, Yoshiharu Tsukamoto and Ryue Nishizawa at the 2010 Venice Biennale, we could view London as a matrix of urban components, and apply a metabolising process that acts as a linking device *'the network of gaps and open spaces within the city'* (Kitayama 2010:23).

Metabolism, meaning *'the chemical processes that occur in living organisms, resulting in growth, production of energy and elimination of waste'* (Crozier 2006) could be applied in urban terms with regards to landscape, viewing the city as a living organism that evolves with the

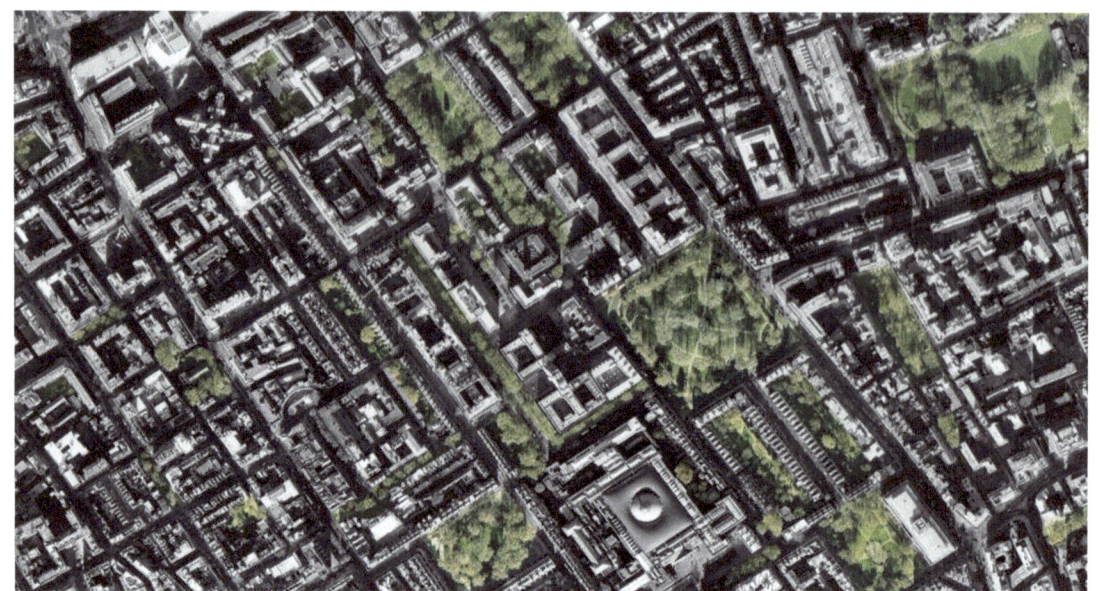

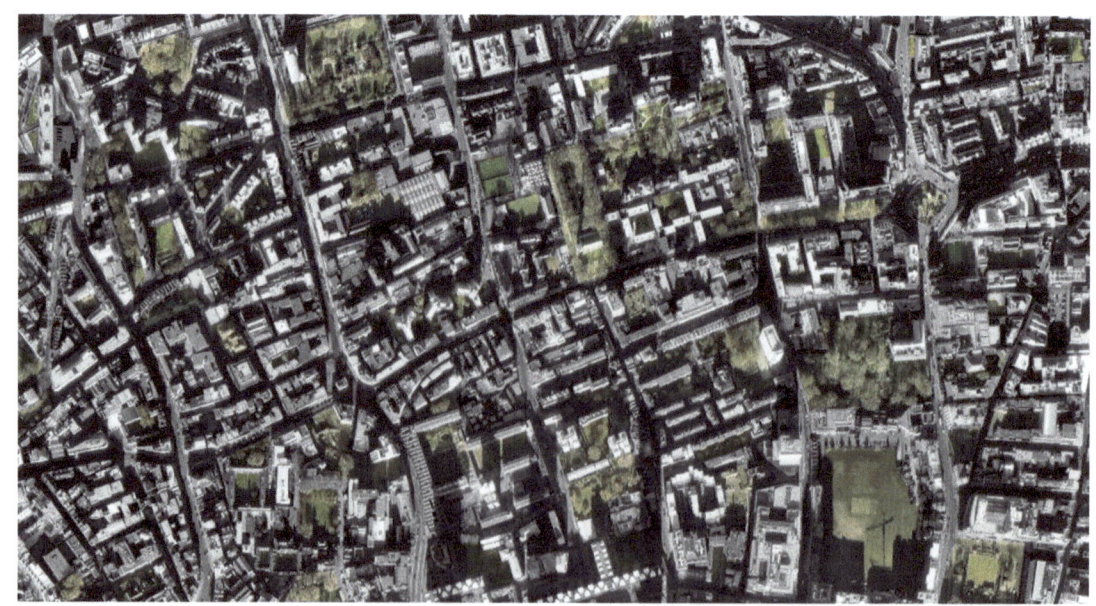

Fig 7 & 8: London's Existing Boundaries and Networks

occupants life cycle. The use of the term 'Metabolism' in architecture appears to have *'evolved [from] designs of plug-in buildings and mega-structures'* (Jencks 1977:9), which suggests the adaptability longed for by Allen in *The Thick 2-D*. Kurokawa would gather contributing architects of the Metabolist movement every two weeks to discuss inspiring projects such as Kikutake's Utopian project City Over the Sea, a series of mega-structures located on an artificial landscape. It was this and other *'utopian schemes [that] gave birth to the notion of the city as an organism which changes at various rates'* (Jencks 1977:9).

The process of metabolising a city might be initiated by simulating the natural evolutionary process of a city's ecological materials and surfaces. The theory of metabolising was to replace the mechanical approach to designing cities with a more organic means of developing changes within the cityscape. Therefore becoming *'an extended biological analogy meant to replace the mechanical analogy of orthodox modern architecture'* (Jencks 1977:9), and a comparison of urbanism to energy processes found in nature; *'cycles of change, the constant renewal and destruction of organic tissue'* (ibid).

Kitayama, Tsukamoto and Nishizawa describe viewing the city's voids as potential for regeneration as *void metabolism*, that is *' based on the grains (or architecture) around an opening (void)'* (Tsukamoto 2010:71). Knowing that these voids occupy the city, they have evolved the architecture to embrace the voids. This concept is not a large-scale, all encompassing urban development plan, but a *'huge mini-development, [that places] the potential for renewal outside the scope of [formal] discussion'* (Tsukamoto 2010:33). By viewing the city one plot at a time, and changing the infrastructure of the cityscape on a micro-scale, the city evolves temporally, creating a redevelopment scheme that can be applied as needed. *'This transform[s] the city into a living organism going through an almost bacterial effect of transformation'* (Kim 2010).

One might identify such a network of voids in London's brownfield sites, and *'It is possible to alter their character both organically and inorganically'* (Tsukamoto 2010:64), reanimating the voids with ecology.
If we learn from the *'Tokyo Metabolising'* model and evolve our cities rather than continuing with a deconstructive-then-reconstructive approach, we can have a more usable urbanism that learns to adapt with social and political changes over time. Miralles and Tagliabue's Santa Caterina Market in Barcelona eschews the demolish and rebuild approach of the city in favour of *'over-lay[ing] new uses, without erasing the old'* (Allen 2002:120) As such, this approach may be applied to

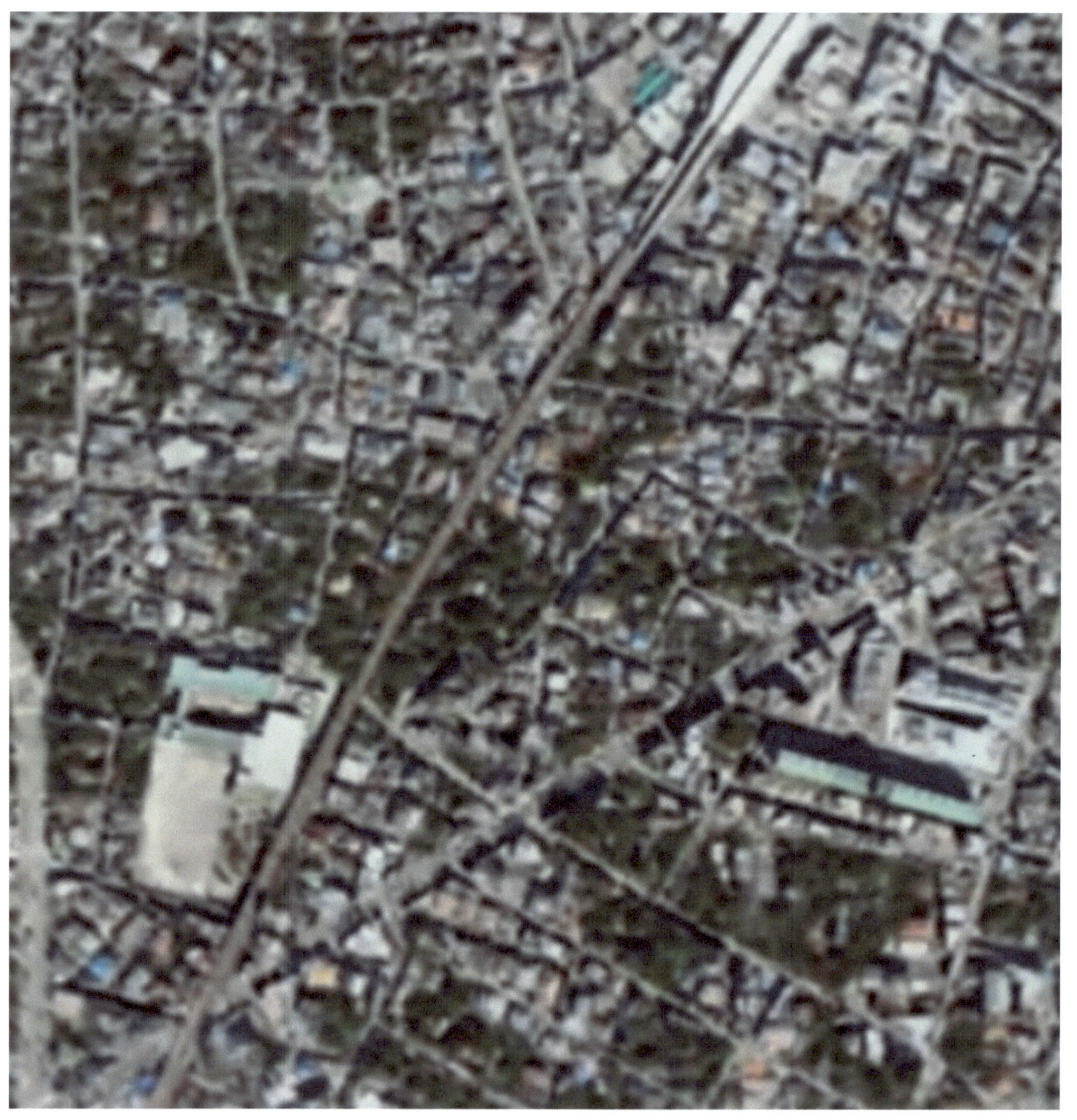

Fig 9: Tokyo Metabolising

ecological as much as architectural actions.

By embracing the voids of the city and blurring the boundaries between landscape and urbanism, we could start to consider a network of in-between spaces that are laid out in a mat-like, horizontal manner, with buildings that are designed for the present by being created for the needs of the community now. We could learn to blend around the existing infrastructures of the city, creating an *'assemblage of non-coincident laminar plates [that] spills out of and around the existing monuments of the city, creating a dense interconnected fabric'* (Allen 2001:123).

Creating structures that blur the boundaries between landscape gardens and architectural structures, much like Junya Ishigami's *Extreme Nature* project for the Venice Biennale 2008, which played with the *'boundaries between interior and exterior [being] dissolved [and] replaced by an unfolding landscape in three dimensions, [where] all is delicate ambiguity'* (Worrall 2008) we might create stimulating potentials for regeneration that could be applied to urbanism, as the flexibility of ecology results in an *'ambiguous mixing of elements form the internal and external environment.'* (Chin 2008)

By *'clearly separating parts of a building or city which have different rates of change, [and] allow[ing] certain structures to remain undisturbed when others wear out'* (Jencks 1977:9) instead of the destructive mechanical process of regenerative urbanism as it currently operates, it might be possible to create a new type of cyclical architecture. This, for me, is the potential that lies in Void Metabolism (Tsukamoto 2010). Therefore, we can prognosticate a new urbanism that might specifically deal with the boundaries between the urban and the non-urban by intentionally remaining fluid.

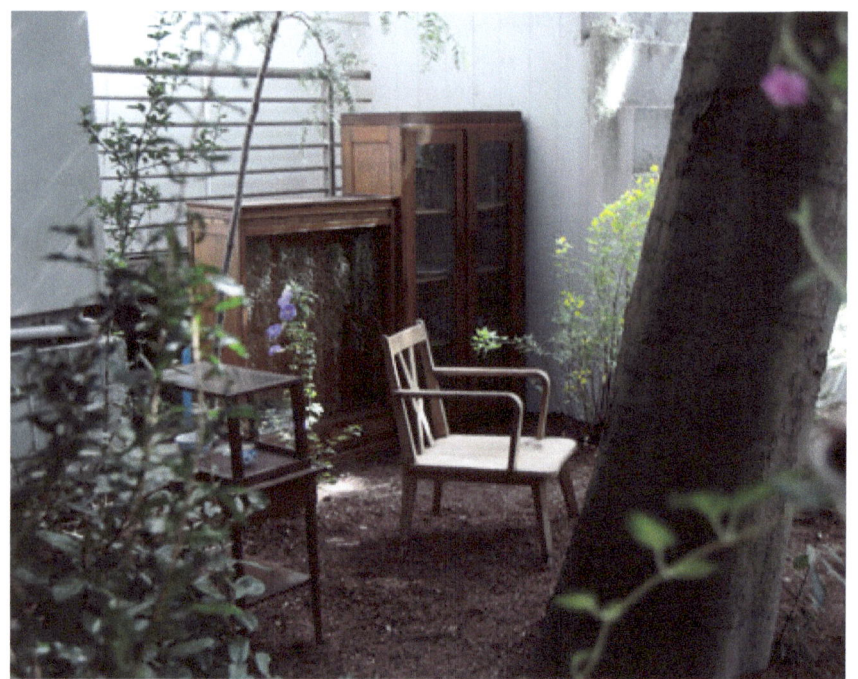

Ishigami's Extreme Nature exhibition at the 2008 Venice Biennale created installations that blurred the boundary of external and internal spaces, blurring ecology and living space together

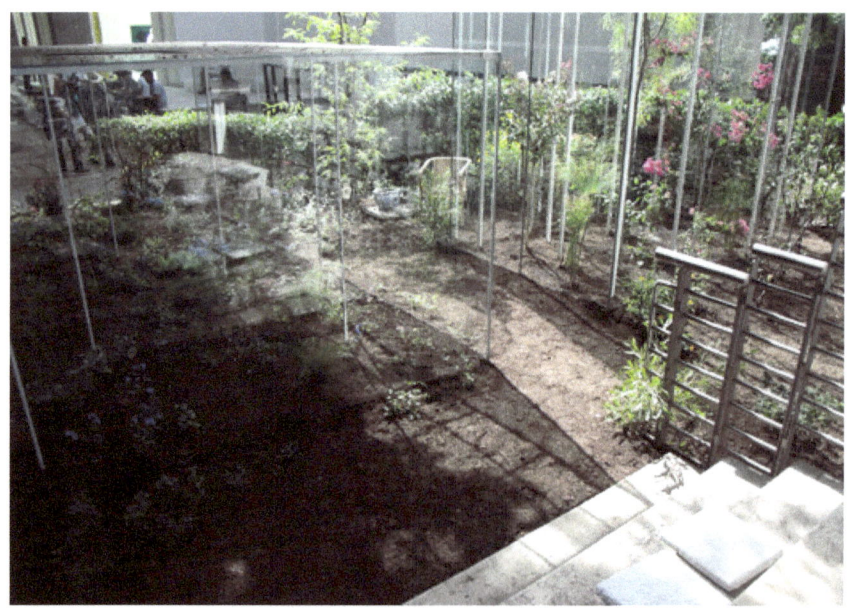

Fig 10 & 11: Ishigami's Extreme Nature

Although the life cycle of an English house currently stands at 100 years (Tsukamoto 2010), the growing population indicates a need for ever-changing housing typologies *'London's population is growing faster than any other European city. More homes at higher densities are needed if we are to meet the increased demand and changing demographics of London's residents'* (Bishop 2007:3). The population in London is set to increase by 500,000 by 2015 and so, *'London has to accommodate huge growth in its population,[…]. Additional new homes are needed at a rate of more than 31,000 a year to give the city a chance of housing them'* (Bishop 2007:6). This will increase the standardised density from *'150 to 500 homes per hectare, called 'Superdensity'* (ibid). With London being dubbed as the most expensive city in the world, there is also need for a diverse hierarchy of residential housing.

Currently, London has a lower urban density than Tokyo, with only 4,795 people per square kilometre. For London to continue to grow and to stay within the existing boundary of the 'Green Belt' the city's growth has *'to be accommodated in an economically efficient and sustainable way, it must optimize use of its available land space'* (Brudett 2007:145). This could be achieved by filling empty voids and occupying brownfield sites, such as old railway goods yards and gas depots that expand for miles either side of the River Thames, which itself forms *'one of Europe's greatest areas of potential expansion and regeneration'* (ibid). By viewing these brownfield sites as potential, positive voids in the city, we might allow London to expand within its own extents, creating an *'unprecedented process of urban retro-fitting that is transforming the image as well as the reality of living and working in London'* (Brudett 2007:19).

Landscape, in the traditional sense, is considered an important part in cityscape design. However, with the use of landscape for mere gestural infilling, the potential of Landscape within urbanism is missed: *'public spaces in the city must surely be more than mere token compensation or vessels for this generic activity called 'recreation'* (Corner 2006:32). Whereas the active blending of the two into a new form of urbanism can offer an *'alternative to the rigid mechanisms of centralist planning'* (ibid), which might allow for a new flexibility to be instigated, using the organic model of Landscape to metabolise the city, changing the existing voids into useful architecture, and for urban programmes to be contained outdoors as well as in.

The blending of landscape and urbanism in London can be expressed and realised in its surfaces, exploring the different layers of the city and

Showing Brownfield sites in London. The black areas indicate the brown field sites, they are spread all over London, many of them found along the river Thames. The Green shows the 'Green Belt' boundary that spreads into London

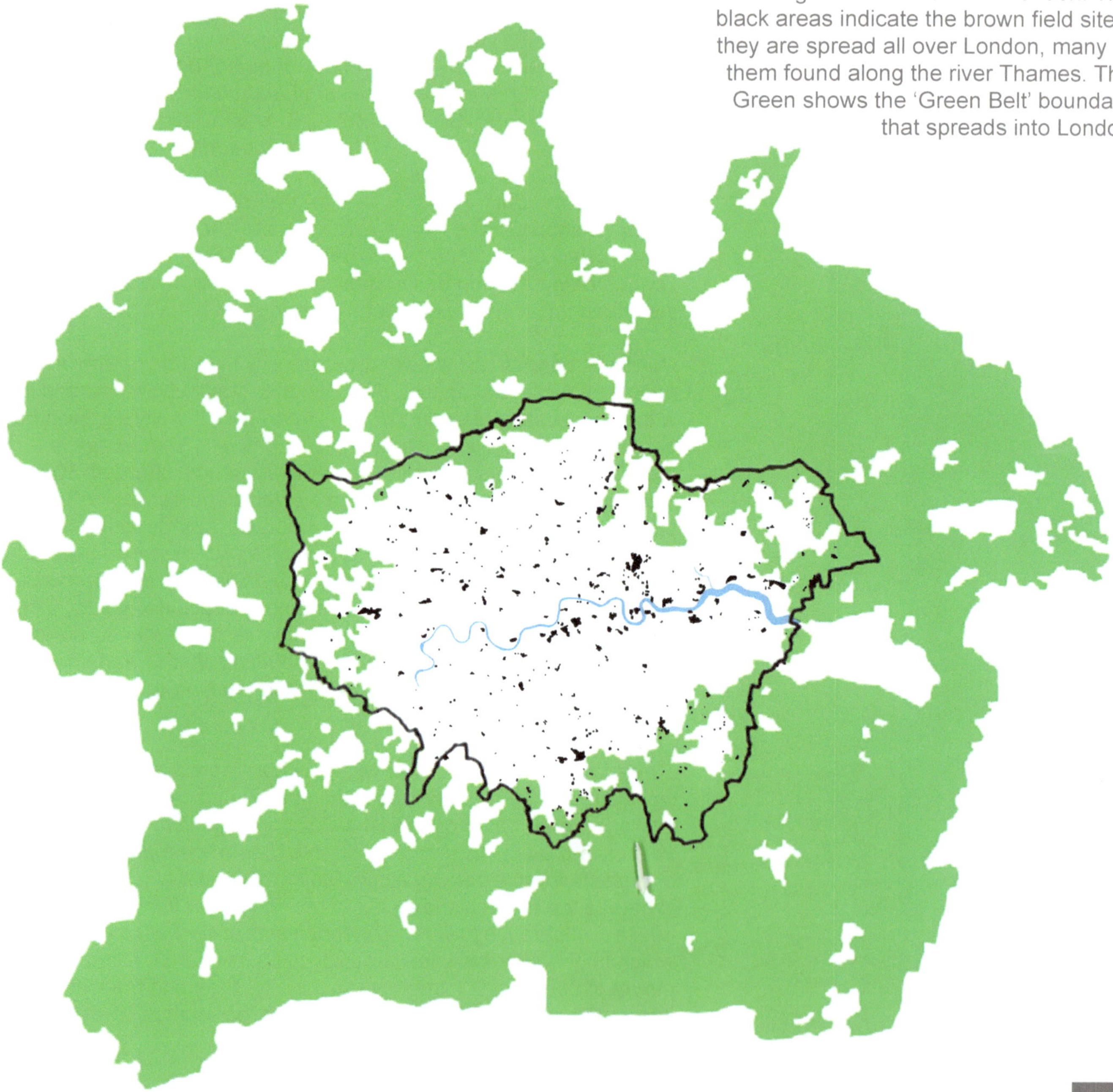

Fig 12: Brownfield Sites in London

15

breaking beyond the horizontal plane. By playing with the importance of surfaces one can view the city in a variation of scales *'from the sidewalk to the street to the entire infrastructural matrix of urban surfaces, [...] where roofs and ground become one and the same; and this is certainly of great value with regard to conflating separation between landscape and building'* (Corner 2006:30). As both an instigator and accelerator of metabolism, surfaces would be *'sculpted to provide a vibrant urban environment for people to work, live and play'* (Naidoo 2009). This is of fundamental importance.

Brownfield sites similar to Bishopsgate Goods Yard could be metabolised for regeneration using ecology

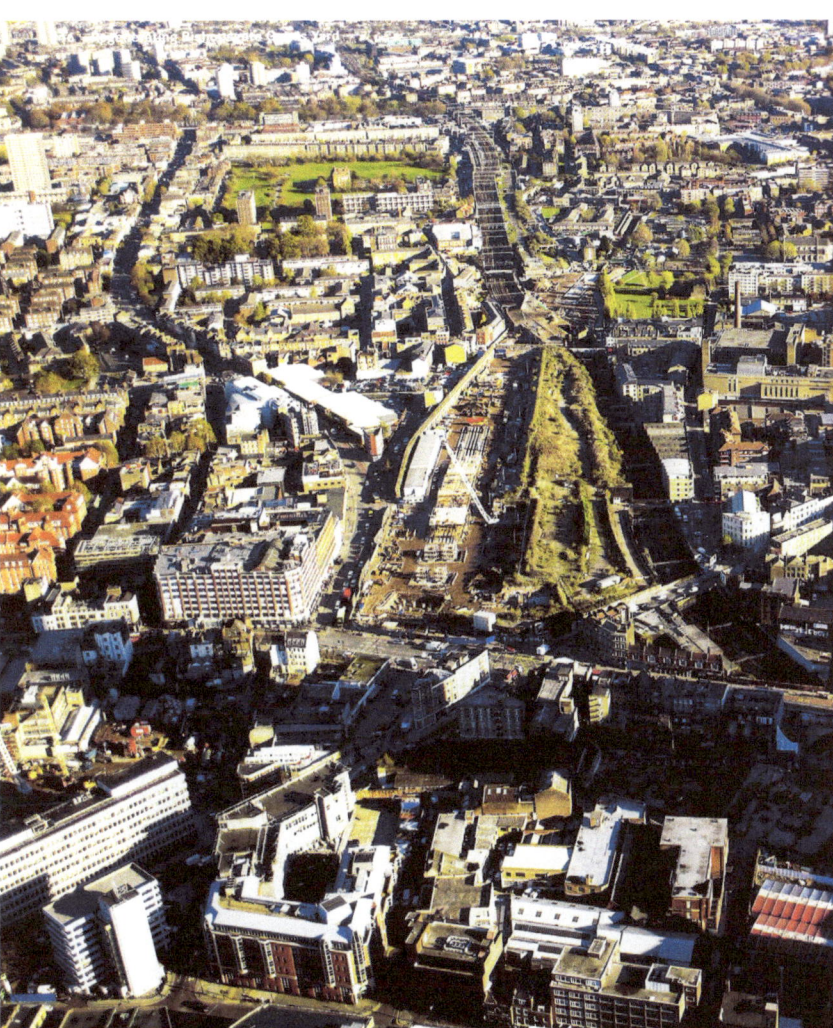

Fig 13: Bishopsgate Goods Yard

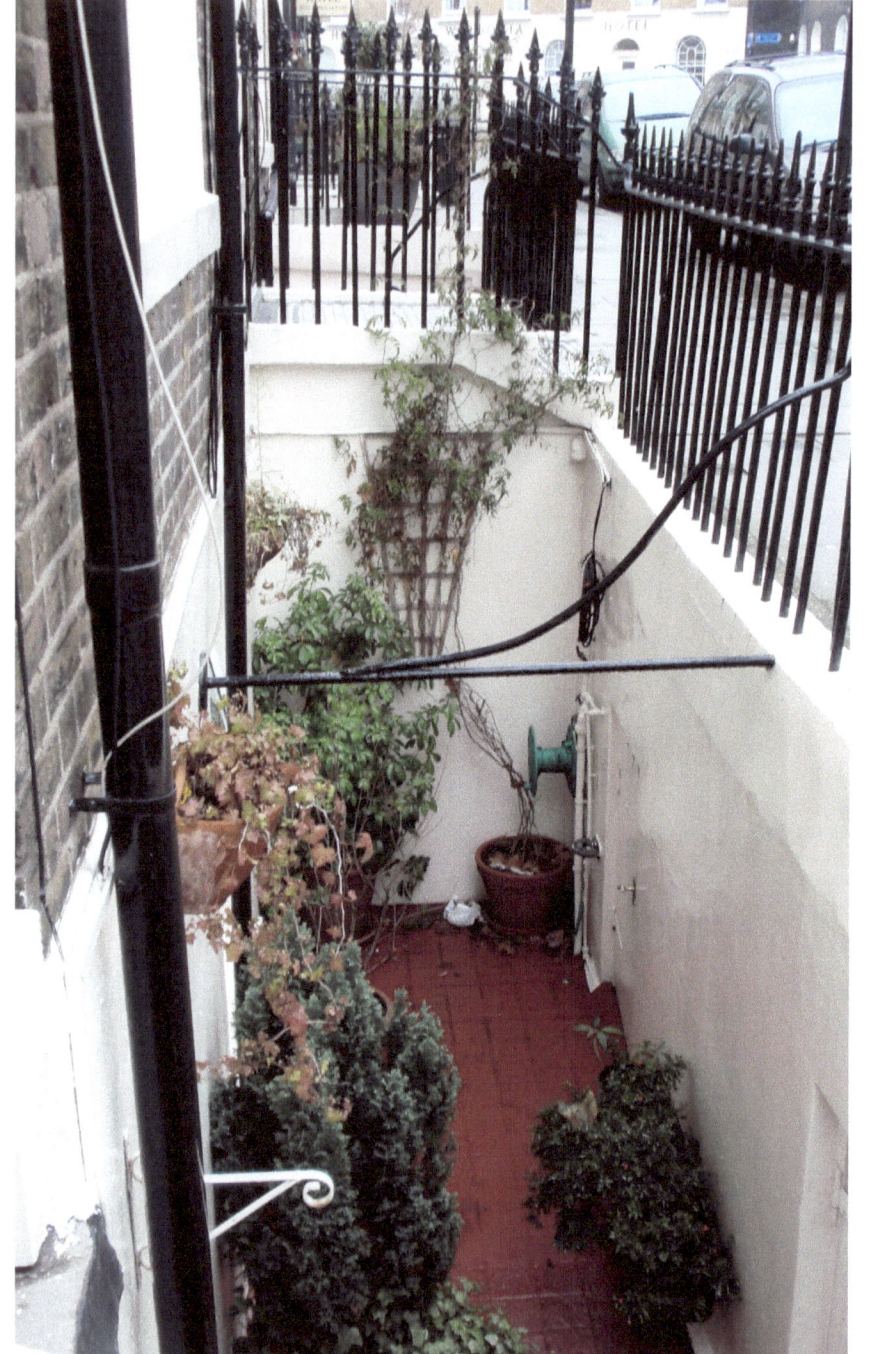

Residents of Cartwright Gardens had begun to utilise basement level voids to create garden spaces.

Fig 14: Cartwright Gardens, Playing With Voids

As has been discussed above, *'London [is] already a city trying its hand at being green'* (Manaugh 2006). It has made some attempts at providing green space in the urban environment. Residential squares containing public gardens and uniform flower boxes introduce ecology into the cityscape. Indeed, Landscape Architect Tom Turner claims that *'terrace housing with gardens is the London tradition'* (2008).

Unfortunately the overzealous pruning and gardening by residents and local gardening initiatives reduces landscape's potential for integrating with the surfaces surrounding it, that which, according to Allen, is *'conceived as artificial landscape'* (Allen 2002:120). Each garden, patio and window box is acting as the face of the household, customised to show the personality and character of its occupant. However, in keeping with the social norm of garden etiquette, the process creates identical frontages to the houses, meaning all intentions of personalisation are demolished. When flowers and foliages are de-headed the act of pollination is intercepted and denied its right to spread. Landscape is therefore 'gardened' to death by the urbanite rather than being allowed to self generate and transform the city beyond the means of civic or urban planning.

Sam Jacob from Fashion Architecture Taste wrote of

'[...] The acres of suburban front garden, each small individual plot tended, weeded, trimmed, edged, paved, mulched, clipped, planted, sown, painted, treated on weekends and public holidays. Between the scale of the individual and the scale of the city something weird happens: bypassing the municipal, evading regulation and beaurocrasy, free of professionals, these miniscule adjustments to the earths crust begin to form grand gestures, mile long skinny strings of parkland woven in intricate knots. They suggest a direct relationship between the scale of the individual and the city: that deadheading a rosebush is an urban act.' (Jacob 2006)

Interesting as the socio-cultural implications of these actions are, the act of gardening is suppressing the potential of landscape, denying it the ability to flourish over surfaces and create a new urbanism that plays with typology and ecology on its own terms.

Cartwright Gardens, a residential square that I recently visited in Westminster, London, demonstrates this clearly. Each house entrance and window is nicely decorated with window boxes and hanging baskets. However, the regimented pruning of the identical foliage crushes the opportunity for landscape to flourish, explore surfaces and expand naturally over the facades, and in time merge with the ecology of the square beyond in order that its residents might be invited to utilise it's adaptable surfaces for living, just as much as they do their own houses.

Opposite the houses there is also a public garden for the resident's usage. The public garden is the Town Planning Authority's concept of bringing *'idyllic countryside'* (Howard 2007) into the city, believing that *'people living in urban areas [want to] maintain contact with the changing seasons. Research has shown that a walk in the park reduces stress and tension, and that a view of landscape accelerates recovery from illness'* (Bishop 2007:25). This leads to most green space being misrepresented as merely pastoral. The lack of use made of the gardens and the obvious over-containment of the green space, makes for an uninviting public area. If the boundary was removed and the vegetation allowed to flourish, an integration between the landscape and its surrounding architecture could start to occur, initiating a possibility for interaction to commence between the pubic and a space that was, after all, intended as communal.

Some residents have started to consider the voids and spaces immediately in front of their homes, which, not unlike in Tsukamoto's Tokyo, *'the voids around the structure allow enough space for a garden'* (2010:63). Residents have used the sunken basement level front patios to initiate landscape growth. These showed potential in using landscape to interconnect different urban levels, but whilst the occupants continue to prune and pot the vegetation, they confine the explorative qualities of their ecological endeavours.

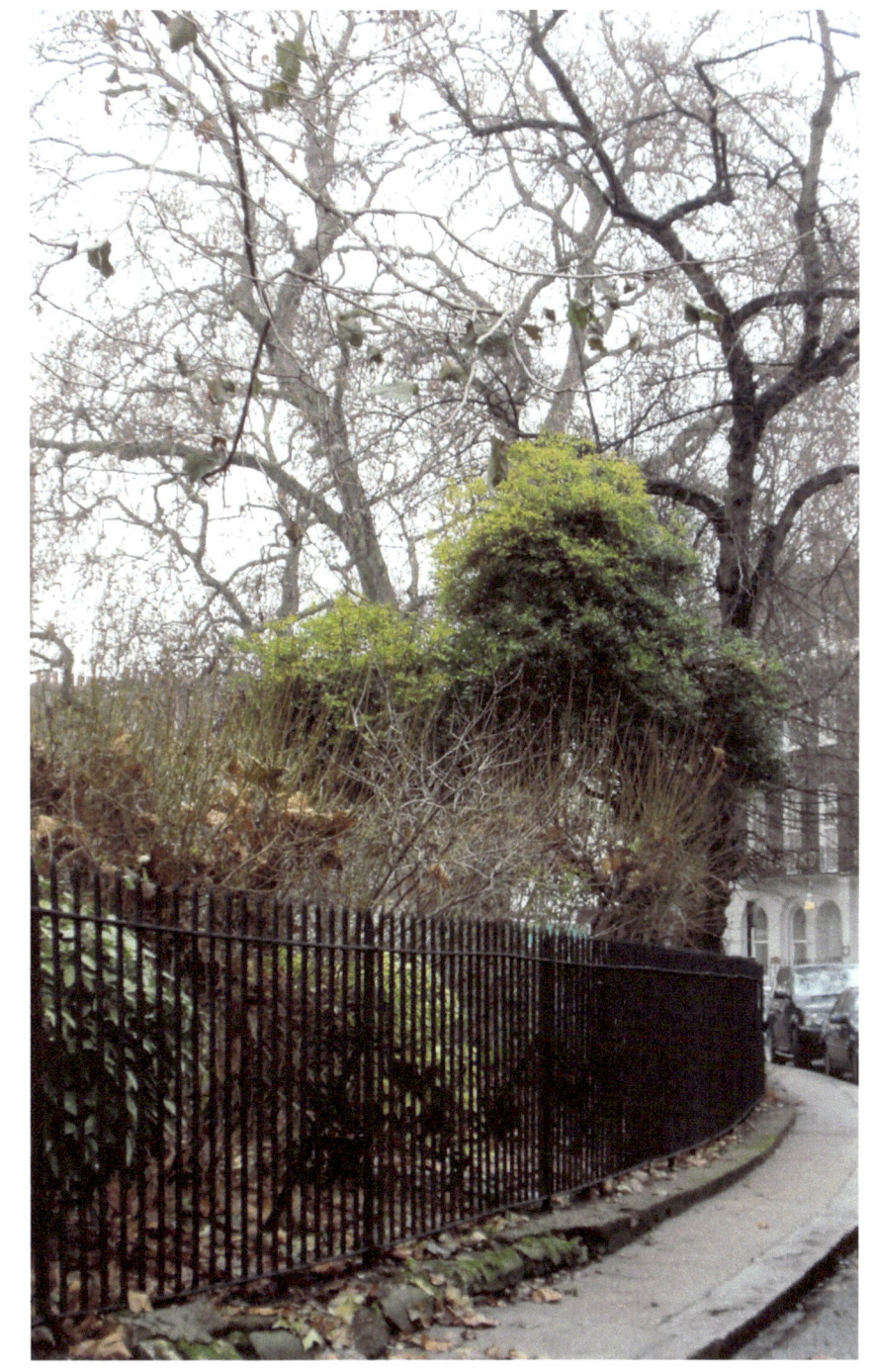

Fig 15: Cartwright Gardens: Iron Railing Boundaires

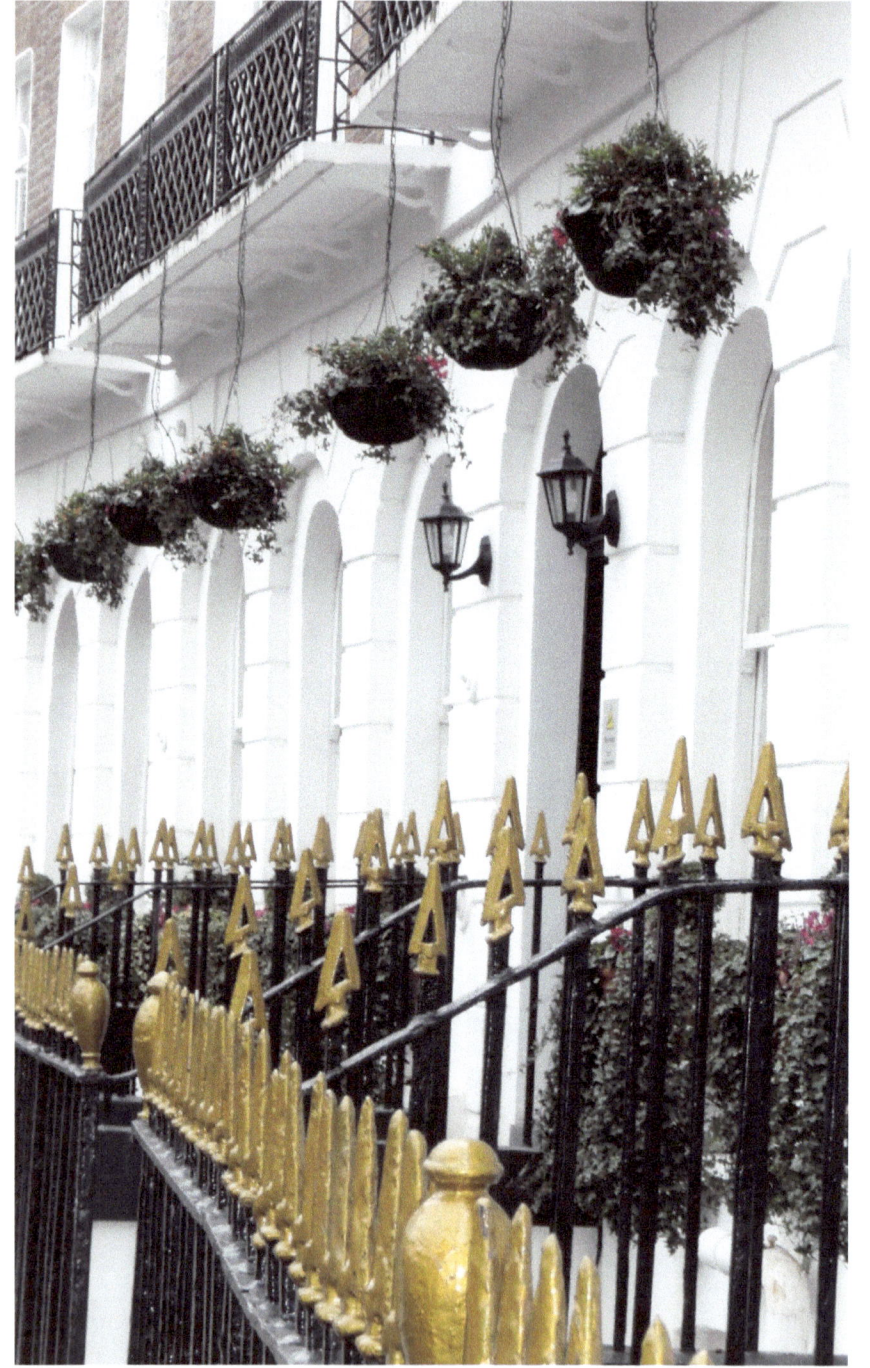

Cartwright Gardens residents had all created matching window boxes, confining the potential of landscape in the city

Cartwright Gardens had strict boundaries around green public space. There is no interaction between the surfaces of the garden and the housing

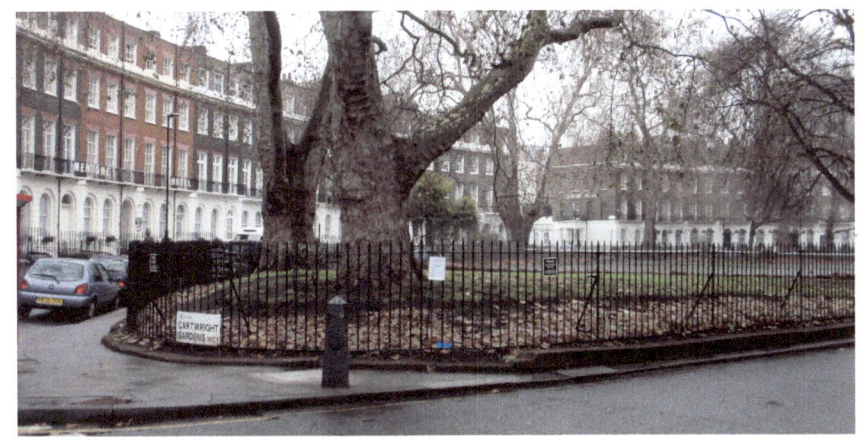

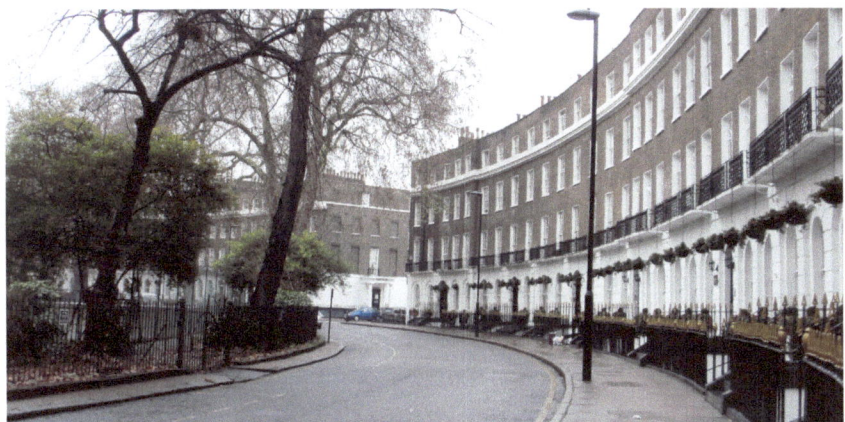

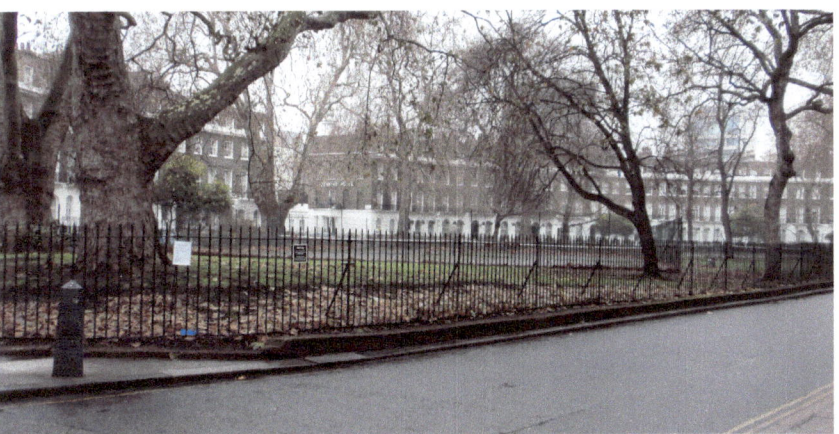

Fig 17,18 & 19: Cartwright Gardens as existing

If the
boundaries
around the
gardens and
gardening were
abolished then
ecology could
flourish, taking
over surfaces
and creating
spaces for
the resident's
interpretation
and interaction

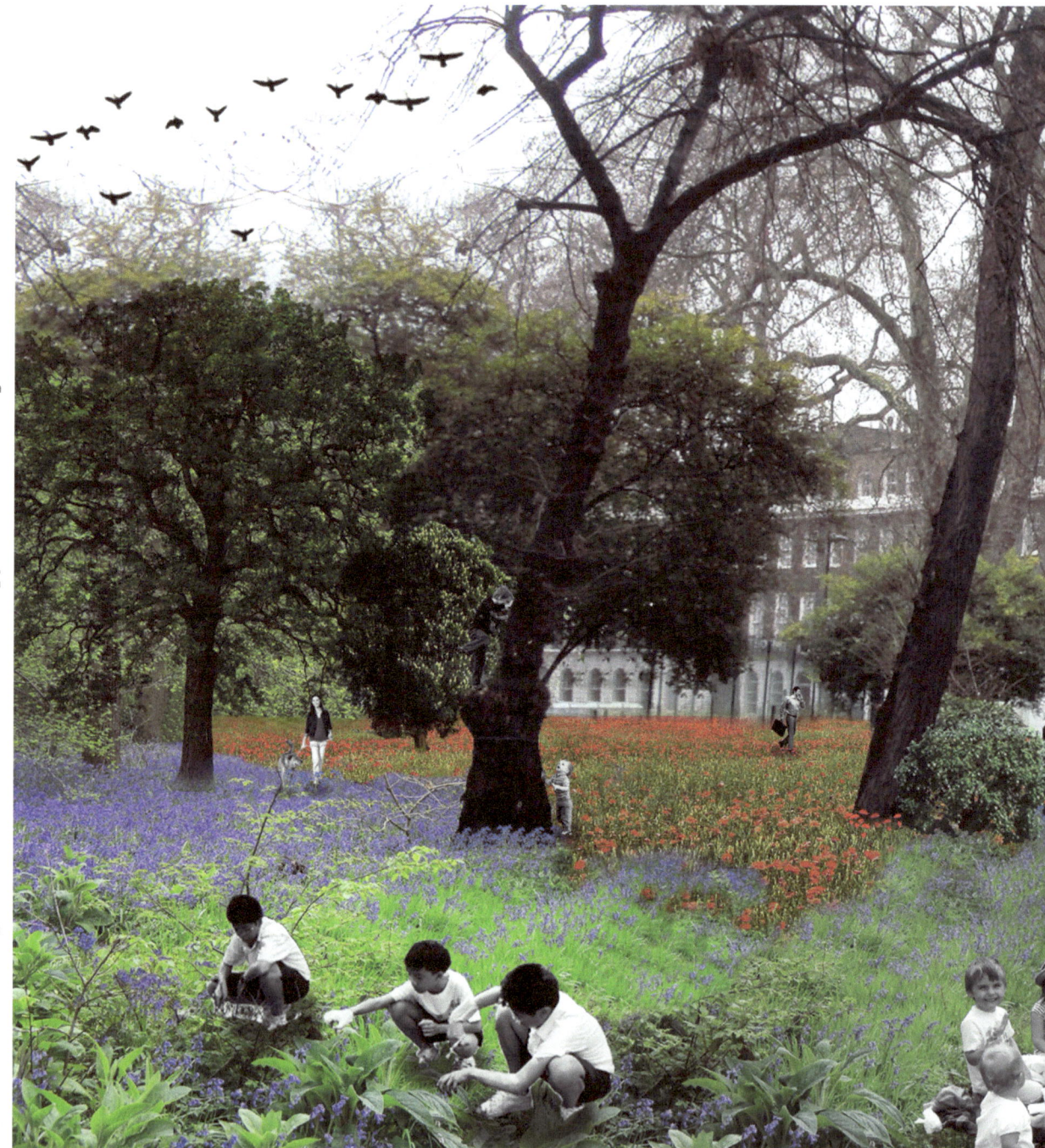

Fig 20: Cartwright Gardens, with ecology flourishing

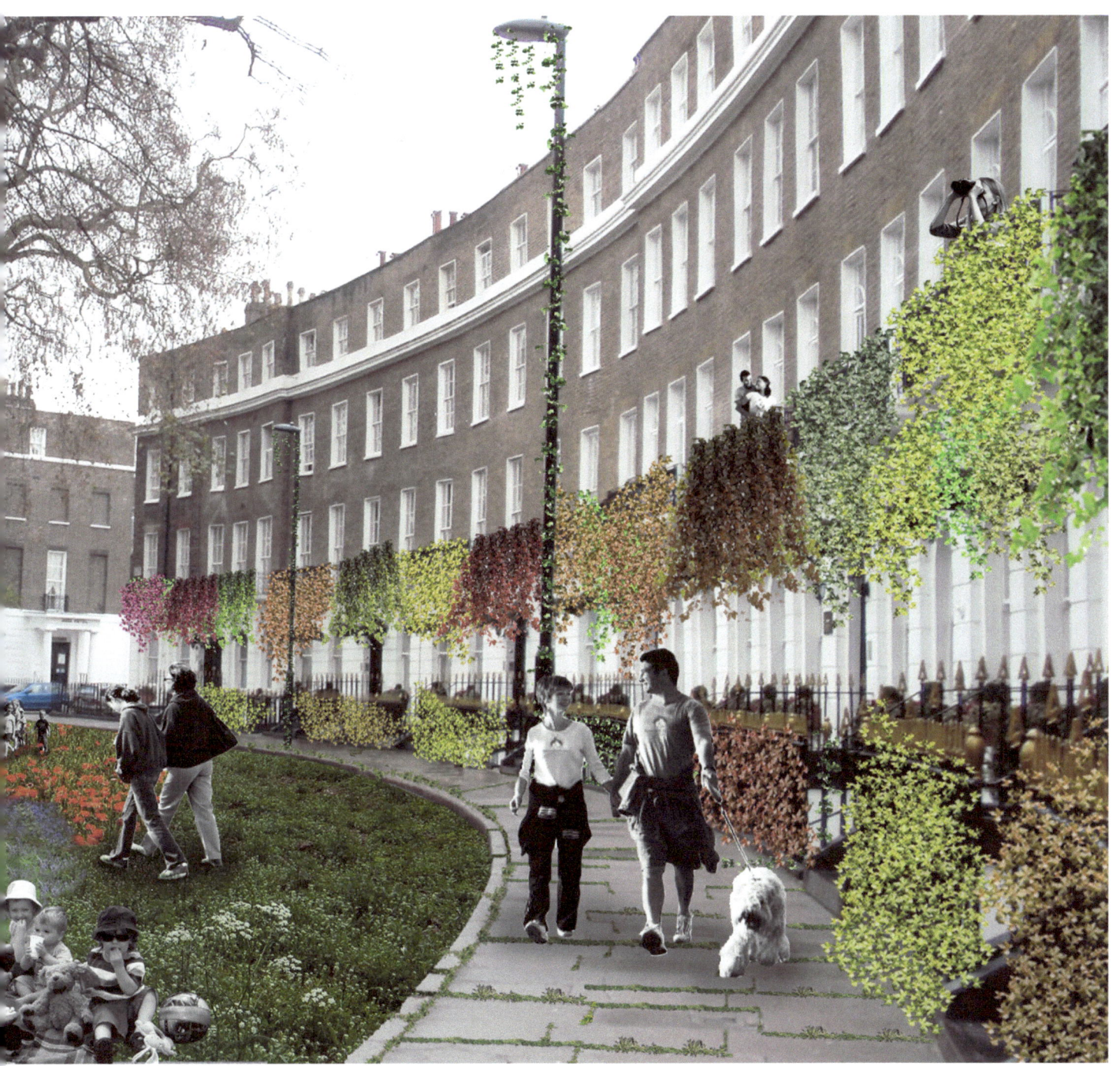

Odham's Walk, Covent Garden, completed in 1981, was a scheme design by Donald Ball as part of the Greater London Development Plan's aim to redevelop Covent Garden. The project was hailed as *'an Oasis of Calm'* (Pye:2007) due to the careful consideration given to individual terrace patios now flourishing with matured plantation that spills over the sides and explores the vertical planes of the architecture. This was something that was not only expected but encouraged by the architect with the *'original artist's impressions not only matched but surpassed by the reality'* (Pye 2007). There is a rich mix of matured planting *'from minimalist austerity through an Italian family's vegetable garden to fiery blazes of crocosmia and pelargoniums.'* (ibid) and this means that even in December, when I visited, there was still a flourish of greenery and ecology creating an 'oasis' in central London.

When walking through the area, one is faced with a maze of walkways and staircases, all leading in different directions, but adding to the tree-top experience when one finally reaches the top level, where there is a mass of multi-layered, topological planting, all situated on the surrounding angular architectural surfaces.

The reason why this project was so successful and forward thinking at the time of its inception (Achieving a Housing Design Award in 1983) was that it was a high-density proposal that still gave the residents the chance to have a garden in an extremely urban setting. *'Given a choice, most families in Britain have preferred to live in a house. Houses have direct access to private outdoor space such as gardens and also empty on to the street where there are opportunities for neighbourliness without enforced sharing of facilities'* (Bishop 2007:14,). And yet, Odham's Walk incorporates high density living with the advantage of private garden patios adjacent to living space, creating a integrated mix of internal and external spaces that encourages urban activities to be played out both indoors and out.

Even though the intention of this project was to introduce landscaping into the urban environment, the project still shows confinement of its relatively fervent planting. Unfortunately, there is a Garden Committee run by residents to patrol the borders of the planters and stop the plantation over running the architecture to a greater degree than it does presently. This I feel is a shame and quashes the exciting promise of the project. If, instead, they viewed the garden and building as *'simply differing intensities of occupation occurring along a more or less continuous surface'* (Allen 2002:120), the planting could be left to play with its own boundaries. It has been thirty years since completion and indeed the plants have matured to create a lavish landscape exploring verticality and layering, but it is my hope that they will continue to do so further. When gardening ceases, what appears at first to be neglect turns into unrealised opportunity. Landscape is allowed to go beyond its original and intended 'containment' and can literally explore the potential of adjacent surfaces for it to bleed into and mediate.

Odham's Walk represents a typical situation where the metabolism of London might begin. Landscape explores voids in the form of patios and open-air walkways, layers in the multi-leveled flats and angular architecture and surfaces with creeping plantation on the walls and spilling over balconies. It also tackles the issue of high-density and affordable housing that is a pertinent issue for London today.

From the streets around Odham's Walk one can see that the foliage spills over the architecture, escaping the watchful eye of the gardening committee

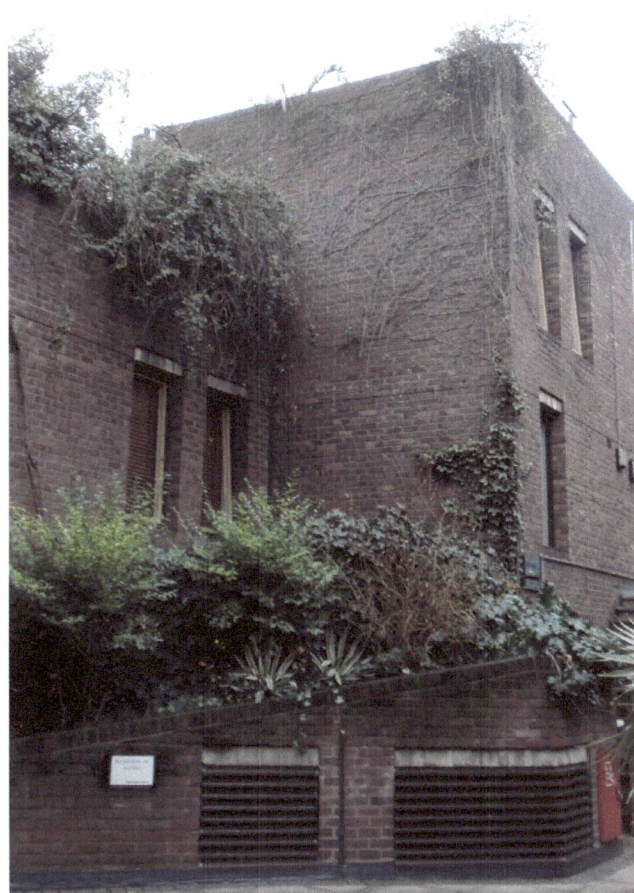

Fig 21: Odham's Walk From Shelton Street

Currently Odham's Walk has a residents gardening committee which keeps the foliage under control. Over 30 years of gardening has created pockets of ecology over the architecture.

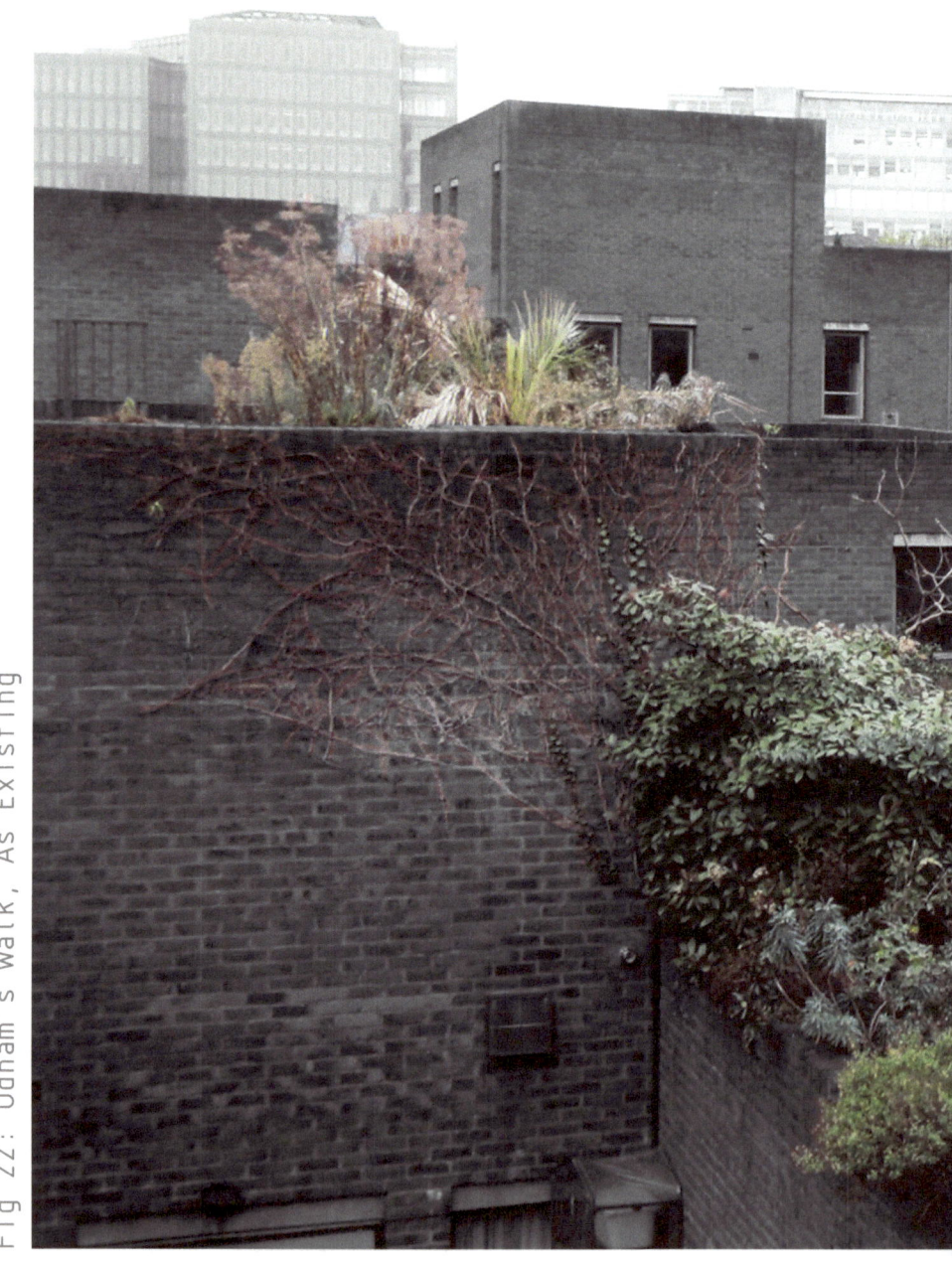

Fig 22: Odham's Walk, As Existing

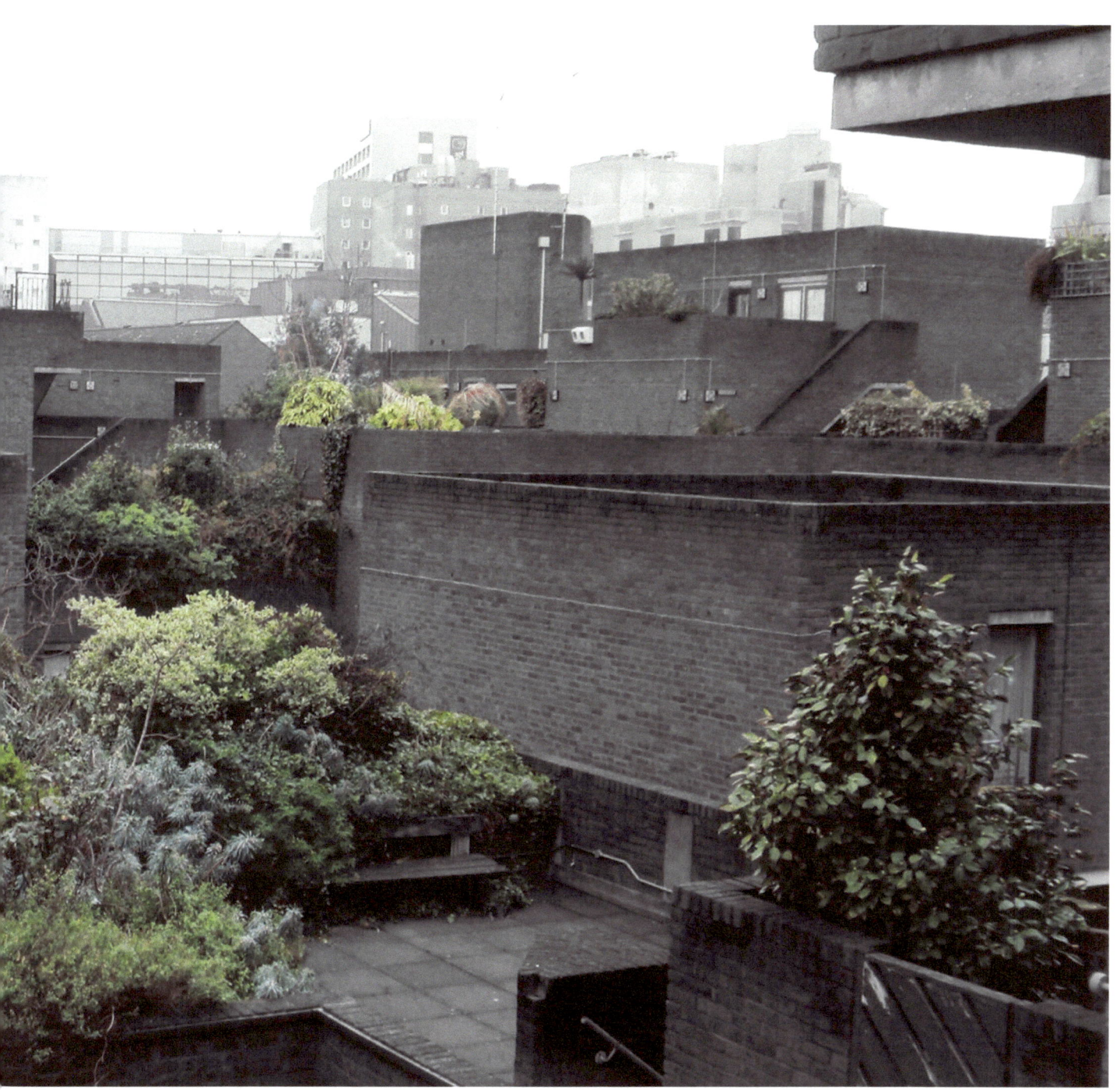

If the gardening committee had never been formed, the ecology could have been allowed to explore the architecture creating surfaces that promote interaction, blending internal and external spaces

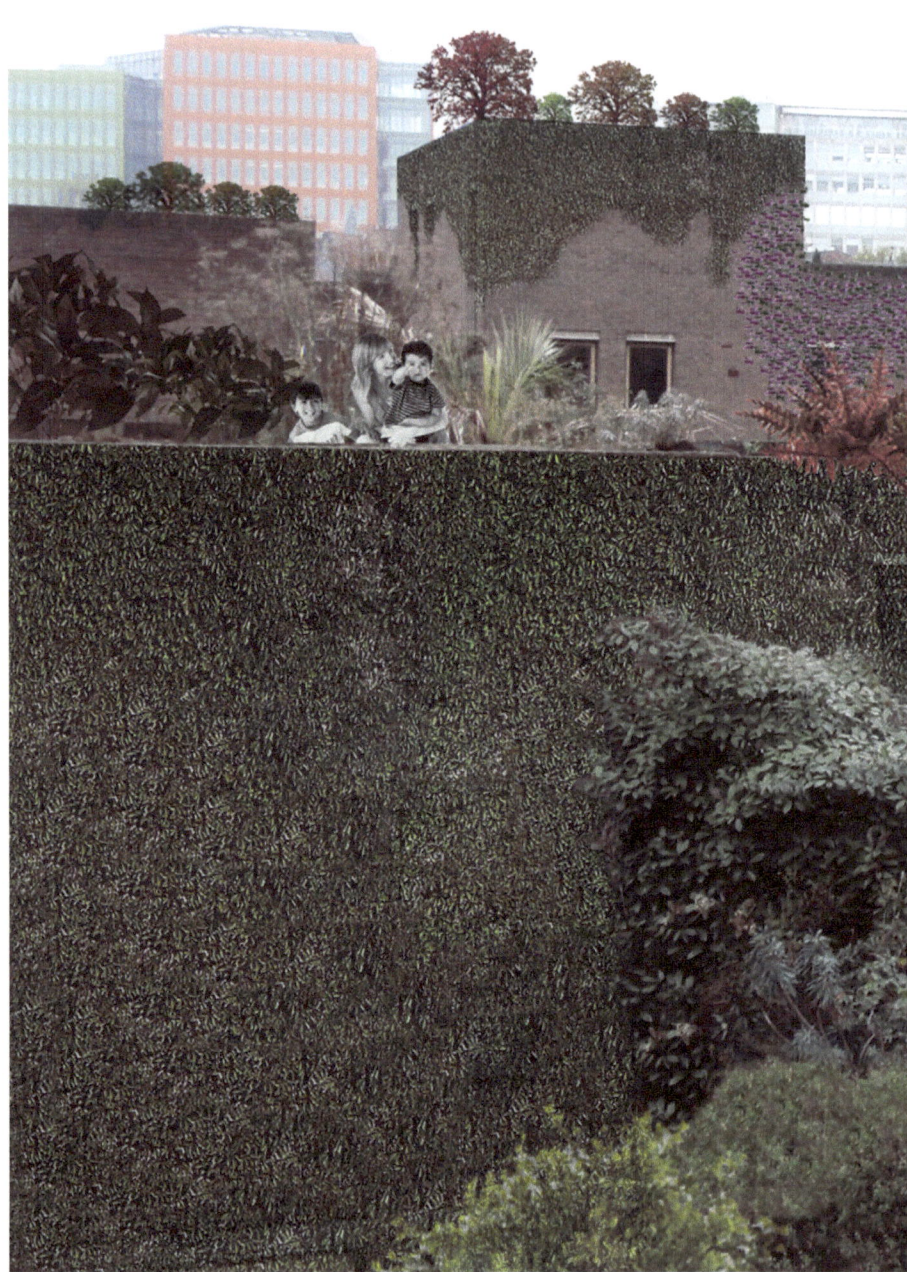

Fig 23: Odham's Walk: Without Gardening Committee

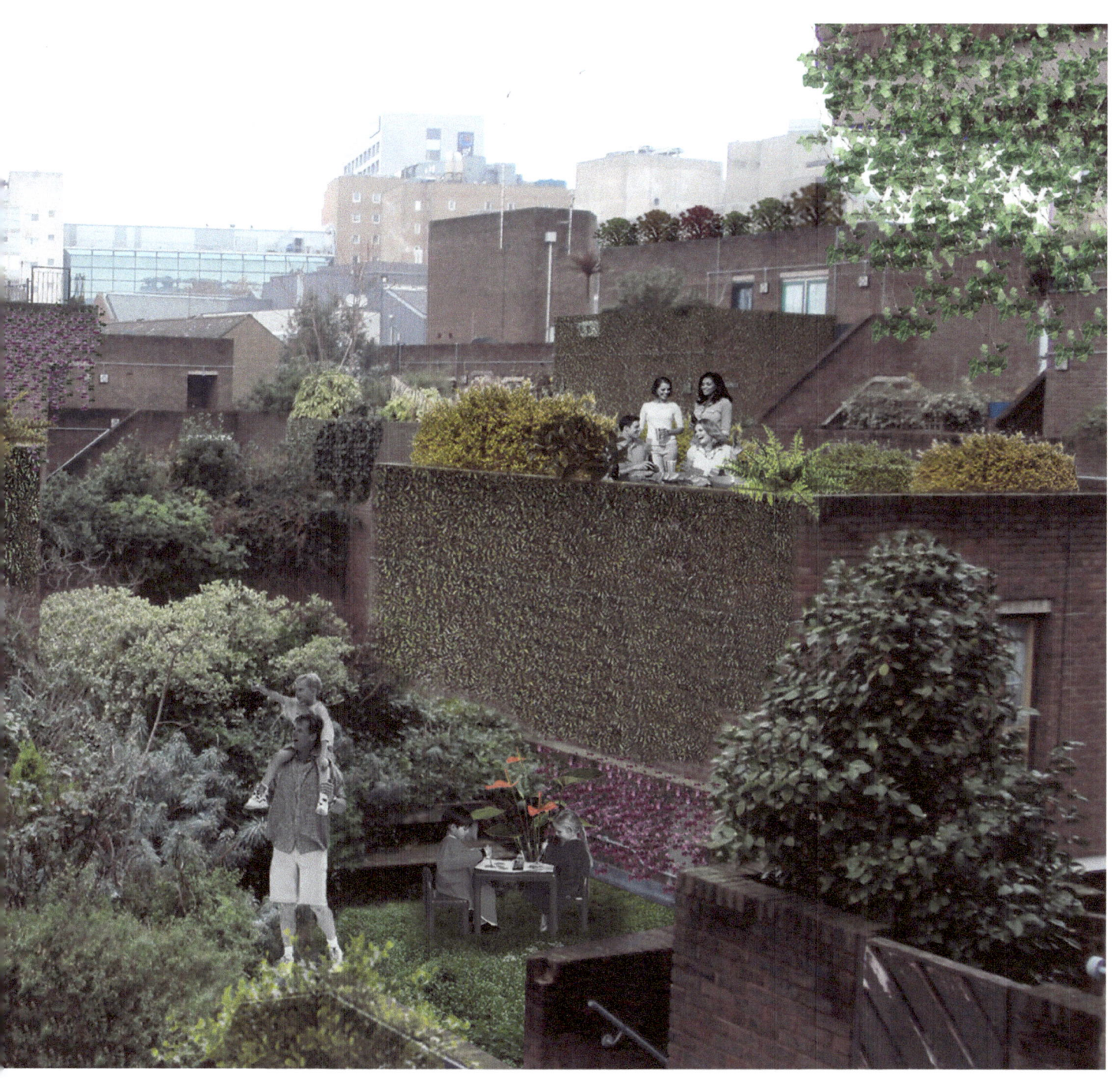

If the act of gardening is abolished and iron railings removed, and landscape can explore the surfaces of the city and abandon its confined territories, public gardens could be left wild to create natural habitats and encourage life, creating *'a choreography of elements and materials in time that extends new networks, new linkages, and new opportunities'* (Corner 2006:31), creating natural landscapes that interact with urbanism rather than fight against it.

Ecology is a flexible model and therefore can change with the city as it metabolises with growing generations; this is important as *'some flexibility is required as to how spaces can be used to suit changing needs and circumstances'* (Bishop 2007:15). With the city expanding and increasing in population, *'the debate is not only concerned with bringing landscape into cities but also with the expansion of cities into surrounding landscape'* (Corner 2006:25). Using ecology as the basis for how to adapt the city means that regeneration can occur gradually, creating public spaces that are not bound by the rules and restrictions of council policies but can be used freely by the public, as intended. A simple patch of grass can be interpreted as one wishes - a football pitch, picnic space, a croquet lawn. However, as soon as one places lines, benches and fences on and around it, it becomes predefined and interaction with the surrounding city is banished. If the surface is left to mature and create its own territory then one can play upon and interpret it as one sees fit, creating interesting juxtapositions in public areas and actively accommodating people's ideas of utopian spaces.

By allowing landscape to blend with the surrounding architecture, spread over horizontal and vertical surfaces, layers of the city and infill voids, *'topological organisation [will then] create a series of surfaces that can be appropriated and modified'* (Allen 2002:120). These modified surfaces can then act as interpretative public spaces that lend themselves to the publics' imagination; *'the architect can design the system, but not expect to control all of the individual parts'* (Allen 2002:122) The city therefore, becomes more playful and flourishes with living ecology wrapping itself between various densities of the city. The line between urbanism and landscape becomes invisible, and outdoor and indoor space can be explored as one. Landscape can be used *'as a unifying model [that] is explicitly evoked in the surfaces that link these scattered functions'* (Allen 2002:121) This creates public interaction and community spirit without enforcement or control.

Once landscape has been left to flourish, we can continue this new ecological model by reanimating the voids in the city and by allowing

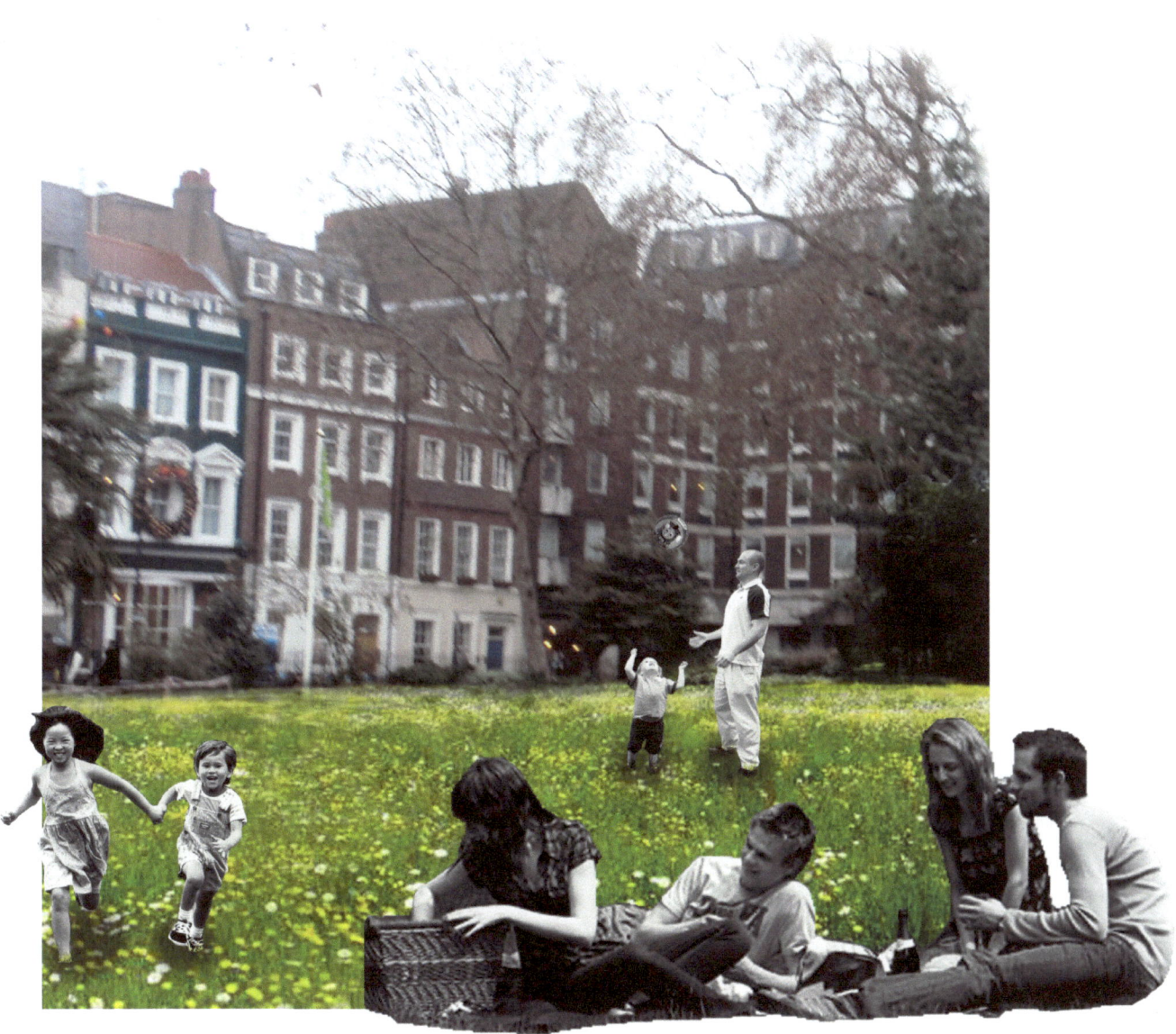

Soho Sqaure, If Boundaries Were Abolished

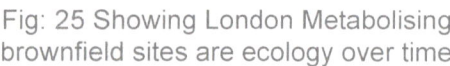

Green Space

Brownfield sites

Metabolised brownfield sites

London's denser infrastructure

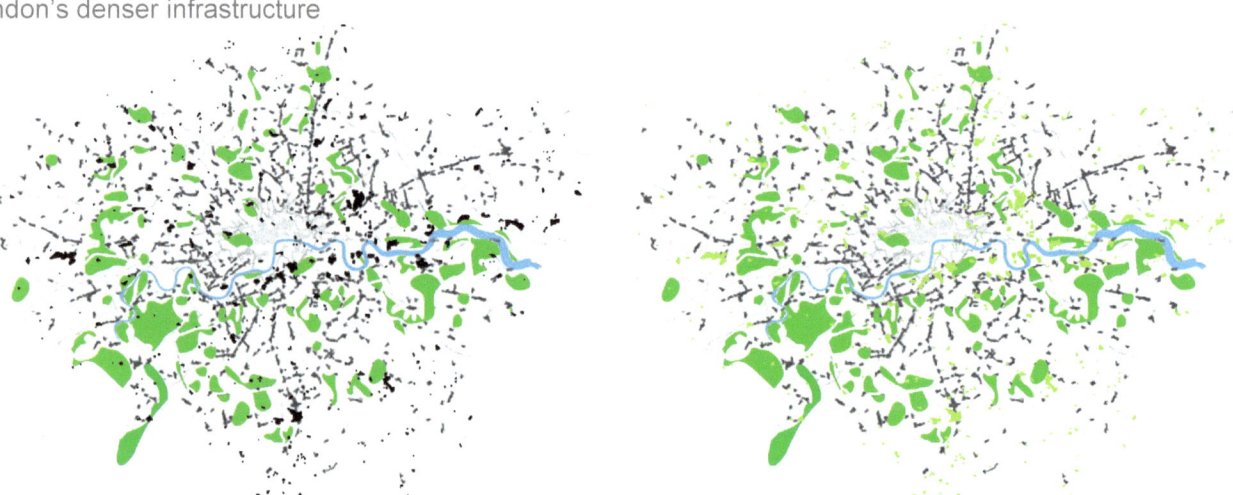

London as it is now, sites are separated with no intergration

Brownfield sites utilised as Green Space

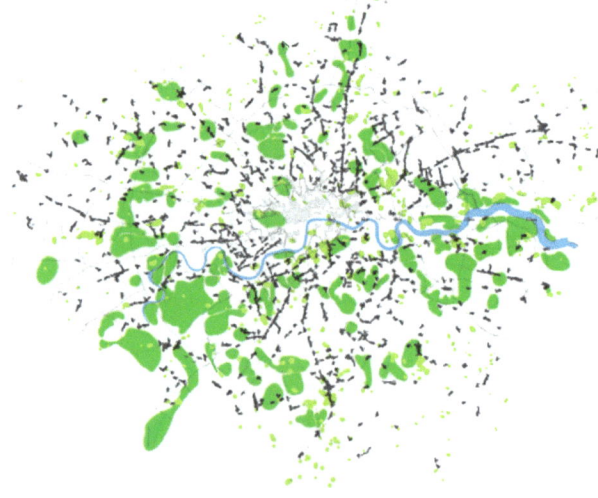

Green Spaces expands due to the abolishment of barriers and gardening

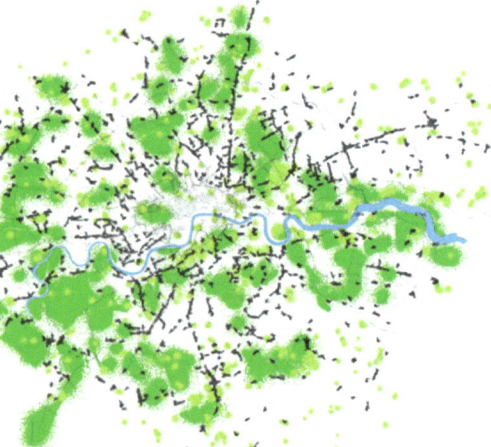

Due to the lack of gardening, ecology is allowed to pollinate creating a city wide spead of foliage

Fig 25 : London Metabolishing

naturally occurring planting and ecological surface to develop: *'it is important to note that landscape is not only a formal model for urbanism today, but perhaps more importantly a model for process'* (Allen 2002:125). Metabolising the voids, one at a time will regenerate the city and adapt it for its future needs without expanding.

At the conclusion of this essay I have come to identify theories of mat-urbanism, landscape urbanism and void metabolism as conceptual apparatus that can be applied concurrently as a means of re-approaching urbanism that utilises the available voids of the city and reanimating them with *'adaptive social ecology'* (Allen 2002:120). I strongly approbate rejuvenation of the city in an adaptive manner, adopting flexibility as an important criteria in the future of our cities, utilising landscape's ecological thickness (Allen 2002) to activate and occupy it in new ways that blur the existing boundaries between ecology and architecture. The hope is for a cityscape that is open to public interpretation and evolves with the social needs and requirements of the city's inhabitants.

Publications

Allen, Stan (1999) *Field Conditions*. In: Sykes, A. Krista. Constructing a New Agenda pp118-133

Allen, Stan (2002) *Mat Urbanism*: The Thick 2D. In: Sarkis, Hashim CASE: Le Corbusier's Venice Hospital and the Mat Building Revival. Prestel pp 118-126

Bishop, Peter et al. (2007) *Recommendation for living at Superdensity* Design For Homes & NHBC, London

Burdett, Ricky, Sudjic, Deyan (2007) *The Endless City*, Phaidon Press Ltd, London

Burdett, Ricky (2007) *The Capital of Suburbia* In: The Endless City, Phaidon Press Ltd, London pp. 145 – 154

Corner, J (2006) *Terra Fluxus* In: Waldheim, Charles. The Landscape Urbanism Reader. Princeton, New York pp.21-33

Crozier, Justin et al. (2006) In: Collins English Dictionary. Glasgow Harper Collins

Deyan, Sudjic (2007) *Governing the ungovernable* In: The Endless City, Phaidon Press Ltd, London pp. 142 – 144

Jencks, Charles (1977) *Introduction* in: Kurokawa, Kisho (1977) Metabolism in Architecture, Cassell & Collier Macmillan Publishers Ltd, pp. 8 - 22

Kitayama, Koh, (2010) *Changing in Urban Areas of Tokyo at the beginning of the 21st Century.* In: Kitayama, Koh, Nishizawa, Ryue & Tsukamoto, Yoshiharu (2010) Tokyo Metabolising pp.15 -27

Kitayama, Koh, Nishizawa, Ryue & Tsukamoto, Yoshiharu (2010) *Tokyo Metabolising*, TOTO Publishing: Tokyo

Koolhaas, Rem (1994) *Whatever Happened to Urbanism?* In. S,M,L,XL, OMA, The Monicelli Press, New York pp. 959 - 971

Kurokawa, Kisho (1977) *Metabolism in Architecture,* Cassell & Collier Macmillan Publishers, New York

Lim, CJ and Liu, Ed (2010) *Smartcities + Eco-warriors*, Routledge, Oxfordshire

Mitchell, William J (2003) *Boundaries/Networks* In: Me++ The Cyborg Self and the Networked City. The MIT Press, London pp. 7-17

Mitchell, William J (2003) *Post-Sedentary space* In: Me++ The Cyborg Self and the Networked City. The MIT Press, London pp. 143 - 158

Electronic Resources

Chin, Andrea (2008) *Japanese pavilion at Venice Biennale 2008*
http://www.designboom.com/weblog/cat/9/view/3909/venice-architecture-biennale-08-japanese-pavilion.html (Accessed 18th December 2010)

Clement, Kevin (2010) On Metabolising
http://intotheloop.blogspot.com/2010/08/on-metabolizing.html
(Accessed on 29th December 2010)

Howard, Melanie (2007) *The homes that the future built*
http://www.hdawards.org/archive/2007/essaypt2.html
(Accessed on the 31st December 2010)

Jacob, Sam (2006) *2000 Years of Non Stop Nostalgia. Or How Half Timbering Made Me Whole Again.*
http://strangeharvest.com/wp11/?p=215
(Accessed on 30th December 2010)

Kim, Erika (2010) *Japanese pavilion at Venice Biennale 2010*
http://www.designboom.com/weblog/cat/9/view/11514/japanese-pavilion-at-venice-biennale-2010.html
(Acessed on 12th December)

Manaugh, Geoff (2006) *London's Green Grid*
http://www.worldchanging.com/archives/004908.html
(Accessed on 29th December 2010)

Mullane, Richard (2006) *Odhams Walk: The Making of a Sustainable Community (Film)*
http://www.designforhomes.org/?act=fil.14
(Accessed on 31st December 2010)

Naidoo, Ridhika (2009) *sturgess architecture: 're- think surface' for vancouver primary*
http://www.designboom.com/weblog/cat/9/view/6430/sturgess-architecture-re-think-surface-for-vancouver-primary.html (Acessed 18th December)

Pye, Graham (2007) *Odham's Walk, London WC2, Historic Winner*
http://www.hdawards.org/archive/2007/historic/odham.html
(Accessed on 31st December 2010)

Turner, Tom (2008) *The Garden and Landscape Guide*
http://www.gardenvisit.com/landscape_architecture/london_landscape_architecture/planning_pos_public_open_space/landscape_architecture_london_lase

Worrall, Julian (2008), *Junya Ishigami*
http://www.iconeye.com/index.php?option=com_content&view=article&catid=415&id=3544 (Accessed 18th December 2010)

Research Blog by Author: http://asliceofurbanism.tumblr.com

www.ingramcontent.com/pod-product-compliance
Lightning Source LLC
Chambersburg PA
CBHW051106180526
45172CB00002B/795